CHALLENGING THE CHALLENGES
Strategies for effective equity and inclusion in education

Dr. K. R. JAYACHANDRAN

CHALLENGING THE CHALLENGES
Strategies for effective equity and inclusion in education
© Dr. K. R. Jayachandran 2023
All Rights Reserved

All rights reserved by author. No part of this publication may be reproduced, stored in a retrieval system or transmitted in any form or by any means, electronic, mechanical, photocopying, recording or otherwise, without the prior permission of the author.

Although every precaution has been taken to verify the accuracy of the information contained herein, the author and publisher assume no responsibility for any errors or omissions. No liability is assumed for damages that may result from the use of information contained within.

First Published in November 2023

ISBN: 978-93-56488-09-0

Price: INR 399/-

Clever Fox Publishing
Chennai, India

Consulting: Kunju C. Nair
Cover Design: Nowshad Kilimanoor
Proof Reading: Saba Sayyed, Aishwarya Jay & Adithya Jay
Art: Sahla Nawas

Distributed by:

Amazon, Flipkart, Shopclues, Clever Fox Publishing

ACKNOWLEDGEMENT

To those who supported my thoughts and activities on different pathways,
To the individuals that challenged me in both my personal and professional life to improve my knowledge, skills, and capacities!
And the Physicians, Therapists, Psychologists, Educators and Specialists in
Prince Sultan Centre for Special Education Support Services, Sinad City of Special Education, Makkah and Saudi Ministry of Education,
Finally, the supportive critics from my own family and society!!!

APPRECIATION

TO MY BELOVED WELL WISHERS

Mr. Gopinath Muthukadu
Dr. Abdullah Al DLaigan
Dr. Sankar Mahadevan
Mr.C.S. Padmakumar
Mr. David Luke
Mrs. Swapna. S
Aishwarya
Adithya

for their enormous support to bring my dream a reality.

Thank you all !

Dr. K. R. Jayachandran

FOREWORD

Equity and inclusion in education is one of the highly prioritized area of every progressive nation. Even-though there have been remarkable improvements in education in India and other developing countries during the past few decades, I strongly feel our country requires quality services for effective inclusion and equity in education to provide equal opportunities, protection of rights and full participation  for every child in our society. The Government of India is in the process of advancing education development by implementing the new National Education Policy (NEP 2020) in India. Our national policy recognizes the importance of creating concrete mechanisms for offering enormous opportunities to provide quality education to various categories of children with special needs.

In this context, Dr. K. R. Jayachandran has penned his new book 'Challenging the Challenges', focusing on identifying the key challenges in equity and education of children with special educational needs in India. I am extremely delighted to see that, he has covered the most important challenges and brought diverse solutions to address such issues, based on his enormous experience in the academics and management of various education sectors in India and abroad. It also gives me immense pleasure to introduce this book as a great source of reference for clinical practitioners, educators, parents, policy makers and all those who are concerned with the education of children with special educational needs in India and abroad.

Though India has developed various avenues for education and rehabilitation support services, we need to ensure the improvement of quality services based on the technological advancement in the rehabilitation sector. The national education policy promotes a national center for quality management in the mainstream education sector and offers high-quality educational services. However, the education and support services of children with special educational needs are yet to be improved with acceptable and accredited quality standard system. Experience shows that majority of our institutions for special needs are not developing suitable policies, procedures and standard of practices to ensure the quality services as needed. As per the inclusive education system, every child should have access to get quality services in their nearby schools. But, our dreams are far from the realities. Our school system including all the stakeholders such as teachers, parents, society, professionals and rehabilitation practitioners etc. should come forward to develop an enhancing and positive support system to bring the best of such needy children and to motivate them to be a contributing member of their community. I strongly believe that, this book can educate all such stakeholders for better understanding and can guide them all to prepare a conducive environment for equity and inclusion of all children with special needs in our progressive nation. The rich experience attained by the author Dr. K. R. Jayachandran as the Rehabilitation Practitioner, Educational Psychologist, Counsellor and a Senior Consultant in various rehabilitation projects in India, Australia and the Middle East, has been reflected in the selection of the topics and detailed analysis and depiction in this book.

I wish Dr. K. R. Jayachandran all the best and success, and I sincerely hope that the book will be beneficial to all readers and contribute to the effective rehabilitation, education, equity, and inclusion of children with special educational needs in every country.

Best Wishes,

Gopinath Muthukadu
UN Celebrity Ambassador &
Executive Director, Different Art Center
Kinfra Park, Kazhakkoottam
Thiruvananthapuram, India

ABOUT THIS BOOK

Dr. K.R. Jayachandran is a rehabilitation practitioner, author, speaker, counsellor and educational psychologist from India who is now residing in Riyadh, Saudi Arabia since 2003. His new book, "Challenging the Challenges" published by Clever Fox Publishing , deals with the inclusive education of various group of children with special educational needs. The National Education Policy of 2020 envisages the idea of including all children in a regular stream irrespective of their disabilities.

This book puts forward the same idea of equitable and inclusive education which is predicated on the notion that no child should be left behind. Dr. Jayachandran envisions a comprehensive plan for including the disability sector to the NEP 2020. Inclusive education, as a concept, when ingrained in every child's mind from a young age helps them become more accepting of the differences between themselves and their peers. Inclusive education helps to remove the stigma attached to disabilities. It helps the abled children to understand the needs of the disabled students amidst them, and become more sensitive towards them with a positive attitude. Disabled students often suffer from low self-esteem issues. Inclusive education can definitely help them to regain and improve their self-confidence. 'Sarva Shiksha' and 'Samgra Shiksha' are the two entities which every educator should be aware of.

Through the eight chapters of his book he gives a comprehensive overview on how the disability sector should be taken care about having good education for disabled children so that they can lead a normal and trouble-free life in their future. His book deals with the challenges and issues not only faced by disabled children but also by their teachers and parents. Early identification and early intervention are the first steps towards challenging these challenges. Every child has the right to education, and that too from a normal school. He outlines a clear plan for this and an inclusive curriculum will definitely help the teachers learn and adapt to this situation. He briefs about the Individualized education plan for children with special needs, at the same time, he highlights about the rehabilitation support services that enables the children to overcome the disorder. The necessary changes should be implemented into the curriculum so that rehabilitation curriculum is adapted to suit the individual students.

He mentions the importance of scholarships and financial assistance for children with disabilities. And for this, apart from the government, he stresses the need for non-profit organizations to come forward and contribute to the financial assistance. In this book he emphasizes the importance of assistive technology which can increase a child's self-reliance and sense of independence.

I recommend this book to all those working in disability sectors, parents, teachers, students and policymakers. The language is simple enough to understand by the common man and I can authoritatively say that the idea is communicated effectively by the author. He never transgresses with NEP 2020 nor does he trespass the code of conduct and ethics in dealing with the disability sector. I am glad to have reviewed this book and wish all success for him. I hope this book will be an asset to all those working in the disability sector.
Best Wishes,

Dr. Sankar Mahadevan
Member, Executive Council,
Rehabilitation Council of India (RCI)
(Ministry of Social Justice, Government of India)
&
Consultant Senior ENT Surgeon
Doctor Sankar's ENT Center
Pottammal, Kozhikode, India.

AUTHOR SPEAKS

I am extremely delighted to introduce my new book, "Challenging the Challenges," which explores the real challenges that students, parents, teachers, and rehabilitation specialists face in our public education system. In this book, I have focused to identify the major challenges in education and providing all possible solutions to address such challenges based on my experience during the last 25 years of  service in different countries. My experience beginning as a teacher, Lecturer, Counsellor, Researcher, and as a Senior Consultant of various mega projects in education and rehabilitation, helped me tremendously to learn about various issues related to inclusion and equity in education. Such experiences helped me find solutions for various issues related to the public education of children with various groups of children with special needs.

The concept of inclusion is based on the equal opportunities of all children to get an education and needful support services in the mainstream public education system. It is obvious that in an inclusive society, every child is equally accepted and recognized along with their peer group irrespective of any disorders, disability, backwardness, caste, creed, colour, or individual differences. However, thousands of children are still encountering discrimination or isolation in our public education due to various reasons. The National education policy of India passed in Indian parliament pledged the equal opportunity and inclusion of all the children in our school system. However, the challenges we are facing still hinders the total inclusion of all the children in public schools. This book 'Challenging the Challenges' tries to identify the common challenges and discusses about the strategies to address the issues faced by the school system in our country.

Various aspects of the challenges in education such as early identification, curriculum management, behaviour management, quality management, and infrastructure development, etc. are discussed in this book with suitable solutions to face the ongoing challenges. The first chapter of this book discusses about the Hardship of school system, parents, siblings, and community in dealing with children with special needs and their families in the public school system. The second chapter 'Early Intervention' discusses about the first step towards inclusion. Types of early intervention programs, methodology, strategies etc. are explained well in this chapter. Consequently, further chapters discuss all the relevant subjects related to equity and inclusion of children in our public education system. To face such challenges, many solutions are also brought to the attention for the parents, students and professionals dealing with children in their education and child development merely based on my experience in the management of education and rehabilitation of children with special needs in different countries.

I hope this book can give insight into all the beneficiaries dealing with our school education system. I strongly believe that, the readers will also accept this book just like my earlier efforts. Waiting for your review and effective criticism to improve my further efforts into positive results.

Thank you all.

Dr. K.R. Jayachandran
1st November 2023
Riyadh, Saudi Arabia

CHALLENGING THE CHALLENGES

CONTENTS	PAGE NO.
Section: 1: Challenges in Equity and Inclusion	13
Section: 2: Early Intervention	33
Section: 3. Curriculum Management	51
Section: 4. Effective IEP for Academic Challenges	67
Section: 5. Challenging the Psychological Disorders	89
Section: 6. Role of Professionals to Face the Challenges	101
Section: 7. Strategies to Challenge the Challenges	123
Section: 8. Quality Management of Equity and Inclusion	159
Section: 9. Appendix : References	181
Section: 10. Abbreviation	186
Section: 11. Synonyms	189
Section: 12. About the Author	191

"Being challenged in life is inevitable, being defeated is optional."

– *Roger Crawford,* Motivational Speaker

Section: 1
Challenges in Equity and Inclusion

Section: 1
Challenges in Equity and Inclusion

Units:

1.1. Classification of Children with Special Needs

1.2. Disability and its Psychological Implications

1.3. Challenges at Early Stages

1.4. Strategies to Face the Hardship of Parents

1.5. Tips to face the challenges

Section: 1
Challenges in equity and inclusion

Life is a journey. We plan a lot before embarking on a journey. We usually have high expectations and enthusiasm, while we plan the journey. We also tend to enjoy the journey till, we reach our destination. We dream about all the ups and downs and visualize enjoying different phases of the upcoming journey. Birth of a child with disability in a family is similar to the condition of a traveler who planned a lot for the trip but realized that we cannot travel as planned. How can a young parent accept that they have given birth to a child with disability or disorder? How can such families survive when they realize that their child is diagnosed with a disability?

However, after a long term of planning, thinking, and analyzing, when we are about to start our voyage, we realize that there are some unexpected challenges in our journey. You realize that you cannot start as you planned, neither can you move ahead on your trip as intended. You may not get the expected support. You may reach an unexpected destination or there may be many unforeseen ups and downs, unexpected expenses, extra help, sorrows, and unexpected upcoming happenings!!!

The ideal parents must be struggling at multiple levels to deal appropriately, when they realize that their child has been affected with any disorder. This is the time of emotional challenge that families might face. It is the time of silent prayer to the Lord they believe in. A time of crucial dilemma that parents find themselves in. Grievances about the unexpected circumstances, the initial stage of accepting the fact, a time of terrible nightmares. What else can a family do!!! This article discusses to overcome the realities of various hardships and challenges of families of children with special educational needs at the early stages of their development.

1.1. Classification of Children with Special Needs

As per the Right of Person with Disabilities Act, 2016, passed in Indian Parliament, following 21 categories are considered as people with special needs based on the difference in nature of growth and development.

As per the various national rules and disability classifications, the mentioned group of special children has been generally considered for social benefits and support services in education and rehabilitation.

Common Disabilities (Disability Bill India, 2016)
1. Blindness
2. Low Vision
3. Leprosy cured persons
4. Locomotor Disability
5. Dwarfism
6. Intellectual Disability
7. Mental Illness
8. Cerebral Palsy
9. Specific Learning Disabilities
10. Speech and Language Disability
11. Hearing Impairment (Deaf and Hard of Hearing)
12. Muscular Dystrophy
13. Acid Attack Victim
14. Parkinson's Disease
15. Multiple Sclerosis
16. Thalassemia
17. Hemophilia
18. Sickle Cell Disease
19. Autism Spectrum Disorder
20. Chronic Neurological Conditions
21. Multiple Disabilities including Deafness & Blindness

1.2. Disability and its Psychological Implications

Researchers are of the opinion that poor appetite, depression, guilty feeling, hopelessness, cursing the partners each other, carelessness, etc. are the common impact generally observed in case a child is found to be born with a specific abnormality in physic or behavior. It is obvious that mostly parents cannot accept the issue and they might neglect the issue, or probably they may tend to develop a negative attitude towards the child, siblings, or peer group due to the stress and depression they are facing. Some of the parents over-protect the child by ignoring the child's future life which may affect the independent life of such children in later stages. It is evident that such situations affect the growth and development of the siblings too.

Shocking Situation

When a parent realizes that their child is having some sort of sensory, physical, behavioral, or psychological issue parents usually panic and are appalled with a sense of helplessness. Such situations make them weak and impotent. They are unable to accept that their child has been diagnosed with disorders. They always match these issues with the other children around them or in their families. Verbal (or even physical) attacks between parents are very common, as one parent may blame the other for similar incidents in his/her family. Either one has to take the blame of having the bad gene responsible for the situation. This situation may impact the parents' marital relationship as well. It can also result in strained relationship between parent and child that might interfere with co-regulated interactions. Moreover, prolonged grieving can threaten an already stressed marriage

> **First step, before you can get NORMAL!!!**
> 1. Shocking
> 2. Denial
> 3. Depression
> 4. Prayers
> 5. Run for support
> 6. Fake Advisors
> 7. Medical Support
> 8. Financial Crisis
> 9. Interventionists
> 10. Assessment
> 11. Acceptance
> 12. Browsing Stories
> 13. Establishing relation with Specialists
> 14. Acceptance (same as 11)
> 15. Attitude
> 16. Crisis Intervention
> 17. Self-Motivation
> 18. Preparation
> 19. Early Intervention
> 20. Starting Support Services

Blaming

Experience shows that parents cannot cope with such situations as most of them are not familiar or have never experienced such peculiar situations in their life. The most pressing question on parents is: What do I do with this child as he/she is not 'Normal'? They feel that their child is not going to give them the joy and happiness as they expected. They are worried about the blame and insult they are going to face in their family. They fear about the acceptance of themselves and their child in the society.

They worry about who will look after their child when they are no longer around? What will be the condition of his or her sibling if the child is diagnosed with severe physical or mental disorders? How can they meet the expenses as it may cost a lot of money to give treatment at this stage? Parents must run from pillars to post! They must cope with the situation by getting second opinions for everyone as they are not familiar with such conditions.

> **Crucial Stages:**
> *This stage serves as a momentary escape for the parents who are attempting to cope with the feelings of guilt and shock.*
>
> **Anxiety:**
> *Anxiety is an emotion, which occurs due to worries, tension, fear, hypertension, and unexpected occurrence in life. Parental anxiety affects the well-being of the family, especially children in their developmental ages.*
>
> **Anger:**
> *During this stage parents may develop anger and it may be directed towards the social workers or professionals who are dealing with parents in the initial stage to offer support services. At times, anger is so extreme that it touches almost everyone because it is triggered by feelings of grief and inexplicable loss that one does not know how to explain or know how to deal with this unexpected situation.*
>
> **Bargaining:**
> *Bargaining stage is considered as the searching of help from pillars to post...., one MD to another MD for expert second or third opinion to cure the health condition that is expected to lead to a specific disability or disorder in the future.*

All thoughts are associated with raising their lovely child just like other children. It is not unusual to see the wife as well as the mother spent after a frustrating day. Some wives accuse their husbands of going to work to escape the non-stop chores. For him there is no other way. He is caught between the disabled child and the frustrated mother. Mostly fathers are the 'fixers' in this kind of situation.

1.3. Challenges at Early Stages

My experience signifies that most of the parents do not understand the disorders at the early stages. Most of them understand the issues only when their child shows delay in developmental milestones. When a parent observes the delay, they discuss it with immediate friends or relatives.

It is so unfortunate that many of the parents do not communicate or share the issue with their near ones. If they discuss it with the relatives, they may comment that this is normal and "Your great-uncle was a late talker, nothing to worry about." or that "The child is just spoiled, you're too lenient with him." Even if they consult the doctor and are getting a proper diagnosis, the family members may ignore the reality, stating that the 'Physician is wrong, and that the child is fine.' It is evident that such parents must be the twenty-four hour a day children's nonstop advocate to state that the 'child is fine'. In fact, some educated parents may browse the internet and may also discuss the issue with others. However, they cannot accept the reality.

Many of the parents deny the issue and some others develop a stereotyped attitude which leads them to being isolated from their own family and society. Unfortunately, some divorce cases are also noted, as the disability becomes a crucial subject, and a parent wants to quieten the other partner by blaming or by finding the reason for disability on the other side of the family.

a. Crisis of Sibling

The crisis faced by the siblings of special children is mostly ignored in many of the families. After the mother, it the sibling who suffers the most due to the disabled child.

If support services are offered to the special children properly on time, the sibling will not have much crisis and both children will enjoy the social interaction and social life equally. If the special child or parents are in crisis due to the onset of disability, the sibling and their peer group also face a lot of adjustment issues in the family. It is very important to understand the common issues faced by the child with disability and their siblings equally.

- Typically, siblings of special children are as normal as any other child.
- Sibling may display attention-seeking behavior as the child with special needs gets more attention than them.
- Sibling may develop a negative attitude sometimes if the special children in the family are over-protected.
- Sibling may lose care and protection in presence of a special child who needs more care.
- More pampering of special children may develop jealous behavior in siblings.

Parents may be busy in their profession for earning their livelihood, and the sibling might be assigned to take care of the special child. The need of the siblings may thus be neglected or ignored sometimes. These situations may lead to the nondisabled sibling missing his freedom in social life with his/her peer group and such siblings may thus develop a negative attitude towards the special child. Affluent parents can make facilities available for both the special child as well as their sibling leading to a positive relation to be established between the two in a most effective manner.

> **Depression:**
> *Most of the parents face the stage of depression when they realize the onset of handicap of their child and the impact it is going to have on their family, society, and the progress of other siblings. Parents are apprehensive about the continuation of their family life.*
>
> **Acceptance:**
> *At last, after approaching all the possible specialists, religious support, social support, and all possible ways, the parent is able to accept the real situation by realizing the strength and weakness of the child.*
> *This is the stage a professional support service can start assessment and early intervention for a child with disability or special educational needs.*

b. Acceptance

Experience shows that it is always very difficult for parents to accept the disorders or disabilities of children in the beginning. They may get wrong information about the upbringing of such children, and may get confused with the strategies of care and intervention that they needed at the early stage. Such parents may be advised to seek the help of a qualified psychologist or an intervention specialist to get proper advice, needful assessment, and essential intervention services. If the parents cannot understand about the need and nature of the special children, intervention services will be delayed, and it will affect the overall development of the child with special needs.

In a study conducted by Sommers V. S. about parental attitudes and social environment on the personality development of the adolescent child, he describes five distinct types of parental attitude. Though, the study is about the parents of children with blindness, this is applicable for all the parents of children with special needs and disabilities.

c. Acceptance of the child and his handicap

Research studies explain that the acceptance of the child is the most desirable form of parental attitude. Though the parents of the special child have mild feeling of bitterness against their misfortune, they do not allow these feelings to over-power them. These parents give special facilities to their special needs child, but do not give special privileges, that may make their other children jealous and ultimately turn them against the child with disability or special needs.

d. Denial

There are parents who have natural love for their special child and do not accept his handicap as a reality. They make every effort and sacrifice for the child just to prove to themselves and others that their special child is no less than their non-disabled peer. They wish their child to compete with and even surpass the peer group and thus force him into over exertions in study and daily living activities.

e. Over Protection

Parents, who forget that their special child is primarily a child and a 'child with disability' later, falls in this category. They overprotect their special child and do everything for them out of their feelings of guilt. As a result, they deprive him of all experiences which are normal to children and are extremely essential for special children as well. Consequently, such child's growth and development may be affected considerably. In such a way, over-protection is similar to a sort of rejection since parents sincerely do not accept the special child's potentials.

f. Disguised Rejection

There are parents who reject their special child but try to compensate for their feelings of guilt by apparent concerns about the child. They try to demonstrate love and willingness to sacrifice everything for their special child. But some of the parents consider blindness as a disgrace and the special child as a burden. There are parents who reject their special child, but try to cover up the resulting feeling of guilt by displaying false concern for him. They put up a show of love and self-sacrifice but covertly consider the disability of the child, as a disgrace and a burden to them.

g. Over Rejection

Under this category fall, the parents who are openly hostile to their blind child and display total and complete rejection of him. They do not pretend to have any affection or love for the child. This attitude may stem from feelings of shame or disbelief in the child's potentials.

Stress of the Parents

Stress is an outcome of physical, emotional, or psychological strain occurring due to various conditions. Long term stress damages the health and emotion of the individual.

Stress of parents of the special needs children varies based on various conditions depending on the severity of the disability and the age of onset of the disabilities. If it is not a visible disability, most of the parents are not much concerned about the early intervention. Visible disabilities such as blindness, cerebral palsy, Down's syndrome, etc. usually get immediate attention based on the visible symptoms at the early stages. However, speech disorders, learning disabilities, autism, ADD etc. may take more time to be understood compared to visible disabilities. Specialist support is highly recommended in case of any milestone developmental issue. Following are the factors

> **Beware of the following**
> 1. *Consanguineous marriage of parents*
> 2. *High risk factors during pregnancy*
> 3. *Excessive medication during pregnancy*
> 4. *Any genetic issues in the parents*
> 5. *Poor or overweight child*
> 6. *Premature birth*
> 7. *Prolonged labor*
> 8. *Anoxia during delivery*
> 9. *Poor birth scores*
> 10. *Developmental delay*
> 11. *Poor eye contact*
> 12. *Poor social interaction*
> 13. *Poor eyesight/ poor eye contact*
> 14. *Poor response to sounds*
> 15. *Being alone and not playful*
> 16. *Poor immunity*
> 17. *Abnormal behavior*
> 18. *Abnormal physical growth*
> 19. *Hyperactivity*
> 20. *Early intervention*

determining the stress of parents when they have a child with disabilities.

- Support of family and society
- Education and culture of the society
- Financial condition of the parents
- Availability of early detection facilities
- Availability of early intervention
- Accessibility to required support services
- Acceptance of special child in the society
- Support and attitude of siblings and peer group

a) Attitude

Attitude of society towards the child with disabilities and their parents is a real challenge always. Attitude is one of the attributes of human behaviour. It reflects the mental and emotional ability of a person and how a human reacts to the environmental happenings. People may develop positive or negative attitudes based on their circumstances, concepts, believes, understanding, habits, and motives associated with a particular person or object. Attitude is the combination of all the life experiences a person faces and it reflects in one's everyday dealings with the environment.

Attitude prepares a person to behave in a certain way towards a specific person or specific class of objects. Attitude of a person towards disability emerges from his/her life experience. A person who is not familiar with a child with disability or a child with special educational needs may not be able to accept or interact well with the child as they do not have any previous experience of the same. So, the positive or negative attitude emerges due to the lack of knowledge or lack of awareness about the nature of people with disabilities. So, attitude modification of people with disability is a challenging task for teachers, parents, and professionals those who are dealing with the education and rehabilitation of people with special educational needs.

Following are the common factors determining the attitude of children and parents towards disability in our society.

b) Adjustment Issues

Parents may feel that a child with disability is a burden sometimes especially the visible disability. The severe conditions such as severe blindness, hyperactivity, deaf-blindness, cerebral palsy, multiple disabilities etc. are more difficult to manage in home settings.

So, such conditions consume a lot of resources and physical energy of the parents, and it causes a lot of stressful situations. Through close observation, it has been noticed that, usually the parents of a mild group of disabilities are considerably unstressed or they are able to overcome the stress through appropriate counselling. Also, it is interesting that most of the parents of children with Down's Syndrome were found to be happy with the children after the initial crisis as such children are more expressive in their love and affection towards their parents and siblings than other group of special children.

So, adjustment of parents with special children varies considering the type of disability, intensity, behavior of children and the intensity of impact on family, living etc.

> **Common factors determining the attitude towards disability**
> 1. *Myths and beliefs about the people with disabilities*
> 2. *Educational and cultural level of the society*
> 3. *Lack of knowledge about human rights and human values*
> 4. *Emotional and cognitive condition of people*
> 5. *Moral identity as a predictor of pro-social behaviors*
> 6. *Lack of acceptance of an inclusive society*
> 7. *Lack of social responsibility towards society*
> 8. *Nature of authority of schools, social institution, and local authorities*
> 9. *Beliefs and religious aspects related to disabilities*
> 10. *Behavior of child and parents*
> 11. *Relation and bonds of individuals*
> 12. *Education and age of individuals with disabilities*
> 13. *Achievement level of people with disabilities*
> 14. *Social and demographic conditions of the society*
> 15. *Role of schools and local organizations*
> 16. *Early intervention*

c) *Challenges of Siblings / Peer Group*

The condition of the children with disabilities may affect the upbringing of other siblings negatively. Especially in case of severe disabilities. Such children need a lot of extra care and attention than their non-disabled peers and parents invariably spend a lot of valuable time on their special needs children. So, the non-disabled peers may develop a feeling of regression as they lack the care and attention that the special child gets from the parents. Moreover, as the parents are assigning the sibling tasks to take care of such children, they may miss their valuable time and may develop negative behavior against the disabled children. So, peer and sibling group counselling is highly important to equip them to understand and accept the children with disabilities among their peer group. Hyperactive and children with behavioral disorders cause serious damage to the nondisabled children and it may cause disruption to the physical and mental health of the sibling at home as well.

d) *Affordability*

If the parents are well to do and are able to support the special children without any financial crisis, they can afford all essential support services at the early stages for the disabled children. Usually, early assessment and support services are costly if there are no free services available for children with special needs. Government and non-governmental organizations are equipped to give many such services free of cost. Unfortunately, all the required services may not be available according to the need and nature of the children considering the peculiar nature of their disabilities. In such situations parents must spend a lot of money on support services, that is a cause of burden for families and such situations cause stress in the family on the onset of disability in a family.

e) *Challenges in Milestone Development*

There are a lot of developmental milestones that children are expected to achieve from time to time during their developmental stages. Parents should be able to understand such milestones at an early stage, so that, they can identify the delay, if any, at the early stages and can provide needful intervention and help the child to achieve normal growth and development. Following are some of the typical milestones to achieve -

- Eye Contact
- Gross Motor Skills
- Fine Motor Skills
- Cognitive Development
- Auditory and Communication Skills
- Social and Emotional Skills
- Behavioral Skills

- o Eating Habits
- o Sleeping Pattern
- o Sensory Development
- o Concept Development
- o Toilet Training

If a child is delayed in any of the above skills, the parents must consult a medical or a rehabilitation specialist at the earliest and do a proper assessment on the functional and cognitive skills of the child. If found affected, needful intervention services should be provided immediately. So that, the child can compensate the skills and develop desirable skills and abilities during the developmental stages.

f) Daily Living Skills

All children are expected to develop daily living skills at the early stages of development. If the child is facing challenges in milestone development or is affected with any physical, sensory motor, intellectual or behavior disorders, it is obvious that the child cannot achieve the living skills. The mother is the first teacher to any child, she is the first person who can understand the skill development of her child. If the child is delayed in achieving milestone development, the child will take a long time to develop daily living skills. Specialized training is required for the child and parents to develop such skills at the home setting. Such skills are essential skills for enrolling the child in school. So daily living skills are considered as pre-school skills. Motor skills, communication, self-care, toileting, and social skills etc. are to be taken care of while we develop skills among children with disabilities. It is a real challenge for families of a child who cannot achieve needful daily living skills on time. A lot of resources and techniques may be required if the child is found to be diagnosed with any disabilities.

g) Concept Formation

Concept formation is incredibly important in early childhood stages, and children with special needs and their families face challenges in developing concept formation among children. It is a hard task to develop concepts if the children have sensory disabilities, especially, children with severe blindness, hearing impairment, intellectual disability, deaf-blind or other multiple disabilities. Research studies indicates that 85% of the concepts are acquired through vision. So, how can a child with visual impairment or someone who is deaf blind understand about the visual clues seen around? The concepts about the color, size, beauty, and concepts on visual clues cannot be formed for children with blindness with the real effect. However, such concepts can be developed in them by using visual clues only. It is more challenging for concept formation of children with deaf blindness. Likewise, many such situations are evident when parents or an early education specialist deal with children diagnosed with disorders or disabilities. Parents and early educators need to be trained in the strategies of concept formation, so that, such children can be trained at early stages considering the peculiar need and nature of their disabilities.

h) *Food & Nutrition*

Research studies indicate that balanced food and nutrition plays a crucial role in child development, especially for children with special needs and disabilities. Autism and hyperactivity are found to be more in number these days as a culture of junk food has developed during the last few years in many countries. Though no accurate data is available about this statement, researchers are claiming for the healthy diet for children in the developmental periods. Consumption of tastemakers, artificial colors, sweeteners, sugar, packed snacks, fries, aerated drinks contain phosphoric acid and carbon dioxide has become a part of the daily life of children and it has shown its impact as behavior disorders, obesity, dehydration, attention deficit, ulcers, cancers and many such challenging conditions in modern families. Such unhealthy food culture has impacted the psychological condition also along with other medical, health, and disability conditions.

Parents are struggling to stop carbonated drinks, and packed snacks that are easily available in all the corner of the world. So, a culture of health and nutritious food needs to be revamped for the healthy living of future generations, starting from childhood. Educating parents of special children about healthy food, appropriate special diet, proper coordination with the health and nutrition specialists etc. are essential for addressing the challenges of food habits among children, especially those with any kind of disabilities. Experience shows that many children with autism spectrum disorders were found to be choosy eaters. So, introducing a special diet may cause additional stress and frustration to the child and the families. Some scientists are of the opinion that a medically diagnosed dietary condition should be followed for children with special needs, especially those who are suffering from Autism and hyperactivity. So, parents and care givers need to be educated on health boosting, developing healthy lifestyles, by following instructions given by the health authority or food and nutrition professionals.

i) Learning Opportunities- Peer Learning

Once parents have realized that their child is having any disorder or disability, Special Schools are the first option for them to enroll their child for education if they are educable. Since long, Special Schools were considered as the only place to educate children with special needs. It is a center where a full-time regular class is available under professionally qualified teachers in special education. Programs such as Speech Therapy, Occupational Therapy, Physiotherapy, Vocational Training, Psychological Assistance, and training in the use of special aids and appliances, are also expected to be available in special schools along with individualized education programs. So, parents believe that special schools are the one point stop over for all the required services.

Unpleasant disability condition at home settings:
1. Severe autism with peculiar behaviors
2. Deaf blindness
3. Aggressive behavior of children
4. Destructive behavior of children
5. Self-injurious behavior
6. Uncontrolled hyperactivities
7. Temper tantrums
8. Unpleasant behaviors
9. Sleep disturbances
10. Uncontrolled Fear
11. Children without bladder control

It is always a real challenge for parents to understand which option is suitable for their child. When a non-disabled child of the same parent enjoys the regular mainstream school, a special child is compelled to be enrolled in a special school. Most of the parents believe that the mainstream schools do not have facilities for their special child, or the child may not get admitted in such schools. Many of the parents do not understand the limitation of opportunities that their special child is facing in special schools. Though, all the support services are available in these special schools, the children are not in contact with the society. Especially the children who can communicate and behave well with others need to develop social skills to be a part of the society. Some children are needed to be kept under constant medical supervision, while periodical examination may be necessary for severely disabled children. To get constant support services special schools are a very suitable option for severe and profound category of intellectually disabled children. But children with hearing impairment, visual impairment and physical disabilities can be integrated along with the normal children, if they do not have severe intellectual deficiency.

This is a real challenge for children, parents, and professionals to opt for the best suitable educational model for their children with special educational needs considering the need and nature of disabilities in the society. So, an orientation about all the possible educational opportunities needs to be provided to all the required parents, teachers, and professionals those who are dealing with children showing special educational needs and disabilities.

j) Early Preparation / Schooling

Early preparation and schooling are very much important for children with special educational needs and disabilities as they are already delayed in their milestone development. This is yet another challenge for the parents to get enrollment in school like their siblings. Usually, a pre-school assessment is a hard task for the parents as the child will be lagging in the expected preschool skills such as milestone development, communication skills, speech, social skills, concept formation and understanding many such essential skills that are expected at the early stages. So, early preparation is highly recommended for the special children for the pre-school preparation. If found affected or in case of severe disabilities, support services should be provided with the support of speech therapist, physiotherapists, occupational therapists, early childhood teachers and related specialists so that the child can be enrolled in a school system as per the same age level peer group.

k) Early Intervention

Early intervention is required in identifying the real problem of the child with sensory, physical, or behavioral disorders if any. Determining the nature of disability, psychological condition, intensity of the physical or other behavioral condition, milestone developments, required medical interventions, identifying the technological interventions, learning condition etc. is essential. Early intervention specialist is expected to provide early diagnosis, assessment, and advice the child/their families, on early childhood disorders and support them to achieve desirable treatment, and other support services at the early stages. In an advanced society all are aware that 'Prevention is better than cure'. Any issues related to a childhood disability should be identified at the early stages and they should be referred to the specialized support for early intervention.

After a proper assessment the required services such as Speech and Language Pathology, Occupational Therapy, Physiotherapy, Behavior & Psychology, Special Education, Family Training and Counselling are to be offered to children/ parents considering their need and nature of disabilities. Early screening of children helps to identify the specific disorders at the early stages of development. Proper intervention programs need to be developed once the problems are identified in the early stage. Our country realizes the importance of early screening and detection of disabilities from 0 - 3 years through the support services centers with the co-operation of nearby hospitals and clinics. Diagnostic Services refers to the early identification of childhood disabilities at the early stages of development.

Medical and rehabilitation professionals are expected to offer the diagnosis services and provide intervention and counselling services so that the child can overcome the disability occurred. In most of the countries the health department is responsible for early diagnosis of childhood disabilities as many of the strategies and techniques in early diagnosis are related to medical intervention. The countries that give high priority to education emphasize early intervention as a part of their educational services. The National Education Policy, (India, NEP 2020) highlighted the importance of early intervention and suggested needful guidelines for the desirable services at the early stages. 0 - 3 years is considered as the early intervention period, before enrolling in any formal education system. Every school system should have the facility to refer the child to a Diagnosis Centre if they are found to be having any childhood disability, sensory, behavior or psychological disorders or delay in milestone development. After a primary assessment of a pediatrician or a designated early intervention specialist, a multi-disciplinary team assessment is highly recommended, if found to be having any sensory, behavioral, or psychological disorders the multi-disciplinary team can take appropriate decision for the required support services. Proper diagnostic services are required for such children for the treatment of physical, sensory, or behavioral disorders.

A Diagnostic Report needs to be issued to the parents to know about the level of the child and for further consultation of the required support services. With such services, on the completion of 6 years a child with special needs can also be enrolled in a formal public education system. In most of the countries early intervention is free of cost. If the child is found to be diagnosed with a minimum of 40% of disabilities, they are eligible to get further concession for treatment and educational services. Parents of the children with special needs may approach the concerned 'District Medical Board' in their district /government hospitals or a state/national institute for disabilities, to get a disability certificate for concessions and benefits.

1.4. Strategies to Face the Hardship of Parents

Various research studies show that at least 5% of the children are facing some form of disorders or disabilities in the modern society. The disorders may be related to learning, psychological, behavioral, and sensory or some other form of physical disabilities.

It is obvious that the parents of such children face a lot of challenges from family and society. Due to the onset of disability a child and his parents may be isolated sometimes. Every year thousands of children with special needs are enrolled in schools. Schools are also facing challenges to address the issues of children with special educational needs.

So, the role of school teachers and social workers involved in the support of children with special needs is increasingly important. The school counselors, teachers, and specialists those who work with students diagnosed with disabilities within their schools, also frequently work with the parents of such students. Such professionals understand the concerns of parents of special children much better than other people. So, school teachers and counsellors can act as an advocate for the parents and students with disabilities to give them proper guidance and counselling for a better education and social life.

Understanding of the challenges and concerns faced by the parents and siblings are essential to work in service of people with special educational needs. So that, one can understand how to support them in facing challenges in their life with disabilities.

1.5. Tips to face the challenges.

35 Tips to face the challenges.
1. Frequent meetings between professional and families and create a friendly atmosphere
2. Accepting the reality
3. Arrange Orientation on child disorders
4. Medical support for prevention of disabilities
5. Support during "Grief & Loss"
6. Positive Attitudes towards the parent & child
7. Avoid labelling
8. Safety concerns
9. Avoid 'over-protectiveness'
10. Family counselling
11. Early intervention
12. Family support group
13. Timely intervention
14. Public benefits and poverty
15. Personal Assistance Services
16. Housing facility support
17. Transportation facilities
18. Health Care
19. Peer Supports
20. Mental Health Service
21. Protection and Advocacy System
22. Support in skill development
23. Volunteer in childcare
24. Family clubs
25. Social workers
26. School support group
27. Volunteers for mobility
28. Highlight the success stories
29. Social media support
30. Linkage with NGO's
31. Unity of institutions working in the field of disability
32. Convergence with local agencies
33. Provide aids and appliances
34. Community based rehabilitation
35. Make pressure on officials to implement laws related to the disabled

Note: Republished Essay of the Author from the book 'Women Empowerment', 2022

*****

Section: 2
Early Intervention
The first step towards challenging the challenges

Section: 2
Early Intervention

The first step towards challenging the challenges

Units:

2.1. Early Detection

2.2. Why Early Detection:

2.3. How to do Early Intervention

2.4. National Education Policy & Early intervention

2.5. Identifying the Disorders

2.6. Early Intervention: Skill Assessment Checklist for Parents

2.7. How to initiate Early Intervention Program

2.8. Management of Early Intervention Services

2.9. Suggested methodology for early intervention program

Section: 2
Early Intervention
The first step towards challenging the challenges

Early identification and intervention are considered as the key aspects of supporting education and inclusion in mainstream schooling. Why such intervention is required for equity and inclusion of children in public education system? This article discusses about various aspects of early intervention services for the benefit of effective inclusion in our society.

Early intervention is the first step of support service program as it is a key component in special education and rehabilitation of children with special educational needs or childhood disabilities. The National Education Policy of India (NEP 2016) highlights the importance of early childhood care and education of children in the age group of 3-6 years of age. So, the basic education activities start from 3 years as per the latest National Policy and it is going to enhance the overall development of all the children especially early learning and overall, wellbeing of children. However, studies shows that due to various level of disorders and childhood disabilities, a large group of children with special needs are not able to be in mainstream due to various disorders or disabilities. Here comes the high importance of early intervention services to detect the disorders at the early stages and bring them to the mainstream of educational sector.

Early intervention is a support service system to identify the early childhood risks, disorders, or disabilities at the early stage of child development. Early detection and early support services are the key components in early intervention services. As per the studies the first 1000 days are very crucial for the child. This is the beginning stage of any child to respond to growth and development in all the developmental milestones. Following are the key milestones of children in the first three years.

- *Eye contact*
- *Fine and gross motor development*

- Physical growth and
- Sensory development
- Speech and language
- Pre-academic skills
- Social skills
- Emotional skills
- Attention and behavior.
- Concept formation
- Daily living skills
- Study skills

2.1. Early Detection:

Generally, early detection refers to the early identification of the childhood disability. If a child is found to be delayed in any of the milestone development, an early assessment for detection of the disorder or disabilities should be manifested so that proper intervention service can be given to the child to make him independent in later stages. The following condition may be suspected that can lead to a disorder or a disability at the early stages of development.

- *Child born to a consanguineous parent.*
- *Child born to parents with genetic disorders.*
- *Child from malnourished mother.*
- *Abnormal medical condition of the parents.*
- *Stress or abnormal psychological condition of mother during pregnancy, especially during the first or last trimester of pregnancy.*
- *Constant consumption of antibiotics during pregnancy.*
- *Substance abuse in parents.*
- *Hypertension, diabetic, thyroids dysfunctions in mother.*
- *Influence of poison, chemicals or exposure to radiation of mother and child*
- *Premature birth.*
- *Prolonged labor.*
- *Anoxia during birth.*
- *Poor birth weight or over birth weight of the child.*
- *Abnormal birth scores and poor health condition.*
- *Delayed milestone development.*
- *Stammering in speech.*
- *Poor eye contact and attention deficit.*
- *Behavior issues and hyperactivity.*
- *Psychological disorders.*

- o *Epilepsy and prolonged anoxia*
- o *Eating disorders.*
- o *Poor in vision, hearing, or poor achievement in concepts formation.*

If any child is found to be diagnosed with the above issues, a professional assessment should be carried to identify the disorders if any at the early stages of the development period. All such issues should be detected and intervention to be started within the first 1000 days after child birth.

2.3. Why Early Detection:

Early detection and early intervention are required to reduce childhood disabilities. Early milestone development indicates the future growth and development of the child. So, growth and development determine the role of families to support the child in a positive way to meet their need and nature. 1st three years are the correction period of the child in case of any difficulties such as health, behavior, cognitive and sensory issues. In addition, following are the key significance of early intervention of children at the early stages.

- o *Early intervention can reduce the critical risks if disorders and disabilities in future.*
- o *Early intervention can help the child to boost the learning skills at the early stages.*
- o *Early intervention can help the parent to be comfortable in understanding the abilities and limitation of the child and support them in a proper way.*
- o *Early intervention will help the parents to reduce the specialized support cost in case they are providing such support at the early stages.*
- o *Child will not have much psychological implications in case of detection and intervention support at the early stages.*
- o *Family intervention and support will be highly effective in case of any disorders.*

Positive reinforcement and interventions are the pre-requisite for future success of the child. So, all the sort of detection and intervention services should be initiated at the earliest so that the child can be treated and prepared for the education without any delay.

2.3. How to do Early Intervention

0 to 3 years are considered as the peak time of early intervention services. Once the child is found to be with a disorder or a disability, the

child should be referred to an accredited professional at the earliest for early diagnosis, detection of disorders if any and provide with needful services immediately after assessment.

Following professionals are considered as the common specialist for the early evaluation and immediate intervention services for the benefit of the children with special needs or disabilities.

No.	Specialist	Expected services
1	Pediatrician	General health and Physical skills evaluation and Identify the critical health conditions.
2	ENT Specialist	Identify the condition of ear, nose and tongue and corrective measures.
3	Ophthalmologist	For proper ophthalmic issues such as blindness or low vision if any.
4	Optometrist	Optometrists evaluate the eyesight, visual acuity, field of vision and prescribe the needful optical and required services.
5	Physical Medicine Specialist	For physical evaluation such as physical disabilities, cerebral pansy, muscular dystrophy etc.
6	Pediatric Neurologist	For neurological evaluation of children to identify nerve disorders, epilepsy and hyperactive disorders if any.
7	Clinical Psychologist	For cognitive, behavior, attention, autism evaluation and follow
8	Counselling Psychologist	For needful evaluation and counselling to get guidance for needed services
9	Psychiatrist	For identifying abnormal behavior and follow up.
10	Audiologist	To evaluate hearing level and clinical intervention for auditory device.
11	Speech and language pathologist	To evaluating the speech delay, stuttering, misarticulation and corrective measures by providing required therapy services.
12	Special Educationalist	Special Educationalist evaluate the learning condition and develop individual education plan based on the need and nature of disabilities or disorders if any.

13	**Multi-disciplinary rehabilitation specialists**	*Accredited rehabilitation specialists in different areas evaluate the strength and weakness of the child and develop rehabilitation services, management of tools and equipment and other related services as required. PT/ OT/ Clinical Psychology….*
14	**Teachers**	*Committed teachers to offer best possible education based on the need and nature of the child.*
15	**Developmental Therapist**	*Therapy specialists from Physiotherapy, Occupational Therapy, Behaviour Therapy, Hydrotherapy etc. can support the parents for early assessment and therapeutic services.*
16	**Podiatrist**	*Podiatrist is a specialist, who provides medical and surgical correction for people with foot, ankle, and lower leg deformities.*
17	**Itinerant service**	*Visiting specialist, who offers home service at the residence of the affected child.*
17	**Clinical nutrition/ dietitian**	*Clinical nutrition ensure the quality of food required for the child.*
18	**Social Workers**	*Social worker is responsible for data collection and parents counselling at the early stage.*
19	**Art Therapist**	*Art Therapist can support the child to develop needful skills in the early stages and support children to overcome learning difficulties at the early stages of development.*
20	**Rehabilitation Psychologist/ Counsellor**	*A qualified Rehabilitation Psychologist service is essential in every stage to support the affected child and their parents in their education and rehabilitation and follow up of services.*

It is a common practice for many of the families that once a critical problem is identified, the parents tend to take the opinion of the grandparents, relatives or a local person from the friend circle, who come to a conclusion about the process of development of the child without any scientific evaluation. Experience shows that such conclusions may lead the child to extreme disabilities or wrong intervention and will affect the progress of the child in due course. It is strongly advised that once the disorder, the child should be referred to the specialist for proper assessment and expert opinion. On time assessment and treatment or therapy can support to reduce the further handicapping conditions.

Parents should not get guidance and information from wrong personnel's and the decisions about the services should not be delayed as this is the crucial period. Also need to take care the quality and qualification of the professionals whom they are approaching for services. Once the child is identified as with a disorder proper certification should be done from the professionals concerned before offering support services for the child. In India, rehabilitation professionals should be accredited by the Rehabilitation Council of India.

2.4. National Education Policy & Early intervention

Along with the early intervention services, early childhood care and education services also needs to be initiated for the affected children so that the child can be prepared for early preparation in education. Early Childhood Care and Education (ECCE) services can enhance the education and development of such children. With the implementation of National Education Policy (NEP 2020), ECCE also considered as an essential component of education of all the children including children with disabilities in India. The NEP 2020 has recognized the challenges faced by children with special needs along with other deserving group of struggling minorities. The NEP recognizes children with special needs and raises concerns to incorporate them into the mainstream education system. It is broadly aligning with the objectives of the Rights of Persons with Disabilities (RPWD) Act, passed by the parliament in the year 2016.

Indian parliament has approved the new National Educational Policy (NEP) in the year 2020. National education policy emphasizes the importance of early intervention and early education as over 85% of a child's brain development occurs prior to the age of 6. It indicates the critical importance of appropriate care and stimulation of the brain in the early years in order to ensure healthy brain development and growth of the child. The NEP also recognizes the importance of creating equal opportunities of obtaining quality education as any other child. Early identification and early intervention services are very important to prepare the children with special needs for early childhood education so that proper inclusion can be established in our mainstream education system.

2.5. Identifying the Disorders

Identification of the disorders in the early stages is the key facet of support services in favor of children affected with any disorders. Family is the immediate contact person for the child. So, it is the responsibilities of the parents and other family members to identify the disorders or disabilities if any by close observation of the following:

- Birth abnormalities if any
- Any delay in milestone development
- Movements of the child
- Eye contact
- Physical growth and development
- Visual responds
- Auditory responds
- Emotional responds
- Unexpected medical conditions
- Anoxic conditions
- Occurrence of epilepsy if any
- Attention disorders
- Poor social response
- Delayed language and speech
- Unpredicted behaviour disorders etc.

Close observation is required to understand any disorders in the above areas. In case of any inconsistency in the growth, development, attention, behavior of the child, professional support should be availed to evaluate the functional level of the child so that parents can understand the actual condition and seek support services to bring up the child like any other children. A checklist is given in this chapter for the family to understand the condition of the child at home setting. Parents are advised to use the checklist to identify the disorders or disabilities.

No.	Details of the Clients/ Parents	√	X
1	Parents of consanguineous marriage		
2	Premature Delivery		
3	Prolonged Delivery		
4	Cesarean section with medical complication		

5	*Low birth weight (less than 2.5 kg.)*
6	*High birth weight (more than 3.5 kg.)*
7	*Diabetic mother*
8	*Hypothyroidism*
9	*The child suffered from anoxia*
10	*Poor birth score*
11	*Uneducated parents who don't care about the management of their baby*
12	*Enormous use of antibiotics*
13	*Stress during 1st or last trimester of pregnancy*
14	*Poor understanding about the child development*
15	*Excessive use of carbonated drinks/ junk food of mother*
16	*Poor milestone development*
17	*Poor physical growth*
18	*Delayed physical development*
19	*Poor social skills*
20	*Delayed in communication*
21	*Poor myth and beliefs about child development*
22	*Frequent occurrence of fever / epilepsy etc.*
23	*Accidents at early stages of development*
24	*Excessive use of screens*
25	*Any odd response of the child*

2.6. Early Intervention: Skill Assessment Checklist for Parents

As explained earlier, identification of the disorders at family setting is very much essential to determine required support services for children and their parents. In this section, various checklists are given as a guideline for parents. Parents or teachers may use this checklist for skill assessment in various areas at home or schools. If more than 50 to 60% items found to be abnormal, the child should be referred to a specialist concerned immediately for further professional evaluation and support services as required. Proper certification also to be done in case if the child to be found as a particular type of disability or disorders.

The following checklist is suggested for the parents, health care workers and teachers those who are dealing with children at the early stages.

High risk factors that are indicated in the following checklist, may show the occurrence of disorders in children at the early developmental stages.

General Checklist at early development stages

This is prepared for the parents to evaluate the child at home settings. If more than 50% items are found to be abnormal, the child should be referred to a specialist such as Pediatrician, a Child Psychologist, or a Developmental Therapist immediately to ensure the condition of the child at early stages.

Observation in the following areas is also highly recommended to ensure the proper growth and development of the child.
- *Early Childhood Skills*
- *Physical Growth*
- *Gross Motor And Fine Motor Skills*
- *Cognitive Skills*
- *Memory And Retention*
- *Behavior Skills*
- *Communication Skills*
- *Social Interaction Skills*
- *Self-Help Skills*
- *Daily Living Skills*
- *Vision Skills*
- *Hearing Skills*
- *Pre-School Skills*
- *Learning Skills*
- *Body Images*
- *Repeated Odd Behaviours*
- *Family History of any Disorders or Disabilities*

In case of any abnormalities in the above areas, it may be suspected to be a cause of disabilities among children at their developmental periods.

2.7. How to initiate Early Intervention Program

There are many strategies adapted and followed by different countries for the successful intervention services for the benefit of children with disabilities. The planning and management of intervention services should be based on the need and nature of the children available in different regions. However, the following are some of the recommendations of the author based on the successful experience of intervention services.

Hospital program for early intervention

Needful facilities to be equipped in all the clinics and hospitals to enhance the early detection of disabilities. District and Taluk level hospitals may equip with intervention facilities. All the doctors, nurses and allied health professionals should be trained in early detection and intervention services. The training program for doctors, initiated by Rehabilitation Council of India is a commendable initiative focusing on this cause. Proper intervention programme needs to be developed along with all the hospitals and clinics. Pediatric doctors and centers should act as a referral points and single point of contacts for early intervention services. The nation realized the importance of early screening and detection of disabilities from 0-3 years so that early childhood disability detection became an important component of national education policy. Child care hospitals, clinics, and Primary Health Centers should have the facilities and accessibility for pediatric evaluation and early intervention in the coming future.

Pediatric evaluation

Early screening of children helps to identify the specific disorders at the early stages of development. Pediatric specialists play a vital role in early identification of disorders. So, training of pediatricians and health workers in identifying childhood disabilities is one of the best ways to initiate early intervention program.

Pediatric specialists should be familiar with the evaluation methodologies and evaluation tools should be available in all the pediatric centers and institute of child health. Vaccination time is the suitable period for disability assessment.

Community Volunteers

Community volunteers can play a vital role in early identification of disabilities. Social workers, community volunteers, Asha workers, members of national service scheme, members of local governments etc. are some of the key personnel associated with everyday activities of community life. If community volunteers are in constant touch with the families, they come across in cases of disability and disorders in their service circle, they can play a role in educating the parents of the affected children and encourage them for evaluation and support services. So needful training should be offered to such community volunteers so that an effective orientation can be mobilized. Early detection of disabilities and child development should be a part of services of all the community volunteers training program in the country.

Early education play school survey

The age of 3 to 6 years is considered to be the early education and early preparatory time for every child. The National Education Policy offers a wide range of early childhood education opportunities to ensure pre-school preparation avenues in our country. So, it is a practical opportunity to identify the childhood disabilities through the pre-school education programs. As soon as the child is enrolled in a pre-school or early childhood education center, all the children should be assessed in their developmental milestones by the pre-school teachers with the help of trained medical or rehabilitation professionals. All the assessment facilities should be familiar to the pre-school teachers so that they can introduce such facilities to the parents. Once the child is identified as delayed learner in any of the sensory, behavioural, communicative or intellectual skills, the child should be referred to the primary clinics or child development hospitals for further assessment and support services.

Kindergarten school screening

Kindergarten schools are the first step to start education. Parents, day care workers, preschool teachers etc. are the main stakeholders in the kindergarten education. All these people are directly observing the child at the early years and they have all the access to understand the skills and abilities of the child during the developmental stages. If any child is to be found with any deformities, they should be referred to proper screening and assessment and evaluation. All the support services need to be enhanced for the child at this stage, so that the child can develop needful skills and abilities to merge with mainstream students.

School screening in the beginning of every school year

Many of the state governments in India have a procedure to identify the disabilities in the beginning of school year. This has enhanced the authority to identify many such children and helped their inclusion and support services in their school environment. This process helps the authority for proper management and budgeting for needful services.

Parents support group

Interaction of parents and volunteer groups became a most effective support system to help affected children and their parents. Non-governmental organizations had initiated many WhatsApp, Telegram and email groups to enhance the connectivity of such parents and it became an effective tool for supporting such children for effective early intervention services. It is the responsibility of every citizen to enroll such parents in community and social media groups. Virtual platforms became an effective tool to connect such parents' community after the Covid pandemic.

Early screening medical camps

Medical camps are one of the best platforms for early intervention services. There are many government and private agencies that have continuous medical camps and awareness programs for medical and rehabilitation services. Such medical camps help thousands of families to identify the early childhood disabilities especially in rural areas.

Referral Services:

Every school system should have a team of professionals or teachers' group who can initiate referral services in favour of the needy children. Disability, learning disorders, behavioural disorders, Attention deficit disorders, Autism spectrum disorders etc. are some of the major areas that need to be addressed through the referral services in the early years of child development. Once any disorder is identified, proper referral services are required to determine the physical, psychological and intelligence level of children to develop proper special education and therapy services at the early stages. In many of such cases a single professional cannot determine and label the condition without an expert opinion. Some time, a local clinic may not be sufficient to provide all the medical evaluation facilities considering the intensity of the problem. Hence it is advisable to refer the child to hospitals or well-equipped clinics with accurate facilities to get proper treatment or expert opinion. A multi-disciplinary professional evaluation is highly advised for any complicated issue.

If further treatment is not required, the child can be redirected to the professionals in the school system. Referral services are essential for most of the children before deciding a particular support service. After getting proper medical or psychological support and report, the school team can develop needful programs in special education and therapy services considering the physical and mental condition of the child. If a resource room facility is not available in school, the school may get required expert facilities from other sources with the support of the nearby resource centers.

2.8. Management of Early Intervention Services

Early screening of children helps to identify the specific disorders at the early stages of development. Proper intervention programs need to be developed once the problems are identified in the early stage. The nation realizes the importance of early screening and detection of disabilities, especially from 0- 3 years of age through the available support services facilities, with the cooperation of nearby hospitals and clinics.

Following are the main benefits of such early intervention services in the management of education and rehabilitation of people with disabilities.

1. To identify the required services for each category of children with special educational needs and disabilities.
2. Develop the data bank of affected children those who need support services.
3. To develop appropriate early screening policies and procedures for the detection of disabilities.
4. Determine necessary facilities with all the technical and human resources required.
5. Develop early detection programs for pre-school and school going children.

6. Identify the children who need medical intervention and develop procedures for appropriate hospital services.
7. Guidance for the follow up of the treatment.
8. Counselling for parents of affected children, their peers and society.
9. Develop awareness programs for the early screening of disabilities and their intervention.

2.9. Suggested methodology for early intervention program

Early intervention services consist of different methodologies and strategies.

Diagnostic Services are the first step in intervention. Medical diagnosis refers to the early identification of childhood disabilities at the early stages of development. Medical and rehabilitation professionals are expected to offer the diagnosis services and provide intervention and counselling services to parents and affected children so that a child can overcome the disability occurred. In most of the countries, the health department is responsible for early diagnosis of childhood disabilities as many of the strategies and techniques in early diagnosis is related to medical intervention. 0-3 years is considered as the early intervention period, before enrolling to any formal education system. Every school system should have the facility to refer the child to a diagnosis center, if they are found to be having any childhood disability, sensory, behaviour or psychological disorders or delay in milestone development. Once the child is suspected or identified with a disorder, the following are the suggested methodology to support for intervention.

1. Observe the child and list the common issues identified
2. Discuss the issues with parents, care givers or pre-school teachers
3. Identify the available facility and professional to get expert advise
4. Refer the child for a proper assessment from accredited professionals
5. Certify the issues for legal purposes and social benefits
6. Medical diagnosis and intervention
7. Therapy, psychological and behavioural intervention
8. Parents and peer group counselling
9. Identify the existing resources for early screening programme.
10. Get the support of multi-disciplinary professional support
11. Identify the available resources locally in distant places

12. Seek the support of government or non-governmental agencies
13. Identify the best national and international practices in early screening programmes.
14. Develop remedial plans based on expert advice
15. Develop the support plan
16. Provide support services with needful therapy services
17. Follow up with medical and rehabilitation support team
18. Early preparation for schooling
19. Provide assistive technology as needed
20. Ensure the inclusion of the child in the mainstream as much as possible
21. Ensure the quality of services in every step of education and rehabilitation of support services for children with special educational needs.

It is the responsibility of the school and society to ensure the welfare of affected children. Through early intervention services the affected child should get equal opportunity, protection of rights and full participation in school and community life.

*****

"Anyone who has never made a mistake has never tried anything new."

– Albert Einstein

Section: 3
Curriculum Management
For Effective Equity and Inclusion

Section: 3
Curriculum Management
For Effective Equity and Inclusion

Units:

3.1. Curriculum

3.2. Inclusive Curriculum

3.3. Factors of curriculum management in inclusive education

3.4. Individual Education Plan (IEP)

3.5. Areas to highlight in an effective curriculum management

3.6. Curriculum Adaptation

3.7. Functional Curriculum

3.8. Curriculum Evaluation

3.9. Aspects of Successful Curriculum Planning

3.10. Principles of Curriculum Transaction in Inclusive Schools

Section: 3
Curriculum Management
For Effective Equity and Inclusion

3.1. Curriculum

Curriculum is the totality of experience that a student is expected to achieve in a learning environment which he is associated with. Through an effective curriculum, it is anticipated to achieve the desirable knowledge from the prescribed syllabus, study from the books, skills development, physical and emotional development, socially acceptable behavior and use of many strategies and techniques required for the learner to be independent in life. All the activities and experiences occurring in the classroom, library, laboratory, activity rooms, playground, virtual platform, teamwork and frequent contacts and discussions with teachers, peer group and friends are also can be considered as a learning experience. As per the ancient Indian scholars "Of all the learning that a student gets, only a quarter of it comes from the teacher; a quarter comes from his own intelligence; another quarter he acquires from his contemporary students and the last quarter only in due course of time!", which means all the experience of the learner is equally important in education environment.

All the theories discussing about curriculum is very much pertinent to the education of children with special needs too. Curriculum planning for children with special needs involves different aspects as the following:
1. Nature of disorders,
2. Functional skills and abilities of the student,
3. Determining the long-term and short-term objectives,
4. Selection of suitable learning content,
5. Organization of content and preparation of individual education plan
6. Selection of learning methodologies,
7. Selection of needful tools, equipments and assistive technology,
8. Evaluation of progress and follow up services in curriculum development.

Experience shows that a customized curriculum cannot meet the needs of a wide range of students' community as the need, nature, intelligence level, learning skills and learning interests etc. varies from child to child. In a structured educational system curriculum is centrally designed for all the children in a certain grade or age group. Such tailored curriculum cannot transact to all the students with special needs together as it does not have the flexibility to address the individual need of the entire children. Consequently, curriculum adaptation is required to address the educational needs of a wide range of students' community in a structured education environment. Thus, curriculum management is a key component in effective inclusive education system to prepare the special needs students to face the challenges in learning and daily life.

3.2. Inclusive Curriculum

In a formal education system, a child with a disability or a student with a special educational need is also expected to learn all the required academic skills for daily life considering the need and nature of the child and intensity of disability. It is obvious that the learning skills and ability of most of the special children is hampered since the onset of disability; however, the needful strategies and techniques are to be offered to support them to achieve proper education and opportunity for mainstreaming. A competent and inclusive curriculum is the basic tool for the effective management of education and skill development for any child in a public education system. Therefore, curriculum management in inclusive education carries equal importance as the effectiveness of mainstream curriculum made for all the children.

This chapter discusses about the need, nature, and relevancy of curriculum development for students with special needs at the primary stages and suggests some practical methodology for effective curriculum management to address their educational needs in an inclusive education environment. It is the responsibility of every school to ensure that the same grade level curriculum, prepared for the mainstream children should be followed for children with and without disabilities, but with proper adaptations like small changes in learning modules, adequate learning environment, appropriate learning approaches, adaptation of teaching learning materials, flexibility in evaluation, etc... All the common learning tools and equipment should be made available for students with special needs too, similar to the facilities that the other non-disabled children are availing.

3.3. Factors of Curriculum Management in Inclusive Education

A well planned, modified, or adapted curriculum can provide better access to needful education for children with special needs in a public education program. A structure individual education plan should be available for every child with disability for effective curriculum transaction. Following factors need to be taken care of in the management of curriculum for all the children with disabilities in the public education system.

- Curriculum management in inclusive education should consider various mechanisms such as early diagnosis, determining the unique requirements of special children, standard grade level syllabus, adaptation of syllabus, lesson plans, preparation of Individual Education Plan (IEP), required rehabilitation therapies, availability of needful special aids and appliances, available support service system required for preparing the child for mainstreaming etc.
- Accessibility for all the children in school and removal of architectural barriers and creating a conducive accessibility plan makes the child comfortable to get the best learning experiences.
- The effectiveness of curriculum transaction is highly dependent up on the dedication of the classroom teacher, teacher assistants, rehabilitation support specialists and follow up of parents, assistants, and siblings in the home settings.
- Considering the curriculum needs effective special education strategies and effective use of special tools and equipment which is equally important for special children in the mainstream school.
- The child should be provided with all possible regular curriculum experience.
- Whenever a child with disability cannot follow the regular curriculum, needful adaptation is recommended.
- Continued and comprehensive evaluation is required in all the stages of curriculum transaction, so that the special child can have needful curriculum inputs as and when required.
- The strategy of curriculum adaptation should complement the strategies developed by the school to address the educational issues of a child with disability.
- Efficiency of teachers and related professionals matters for the effectiveness of curriculum adaptation

- ○ Standard curriculum should consider the age, skills, intelligence, physical condition, mental level, and learning readiness of the child.
- ○ Curriculum should be need-based and should be functional to change the behavioral and functional skill level of the child.

3.4. Individual Education Plan (IEP)

IEP is considered as the most important implementation document in the education and rehabilitation support of children with special educational needs. For every support service, the child needs proper planning and documentation, explaining the procedure and process of services rendered for the overall development of the student with special needs. IEP can be described as a syllabus that has been designed for students with disabilities with a specific purpose and which includes a modified version of a school curriculum along with the required rehabilitation services.

IEP is expected to prepare the team of specialists in cooperation with the parents and teachers those who are associated with the student's progress. In general teachers, a case manager, parents, specialist staff, school counsellors, community specialists and wherever possible, the students themselves are the key stakeholders in IEP planning. IEP should be a mandatory document to all the students with special needs who have disabilities of an intellectual, physical, sensory, emotional or behavioural nature, or who have exceptional gifts or talents. All such children need separate planning and management of education and rehabilitation services considering the need and nature of peculiar disabilities.

Following are the Key Methodologies of managing a standard IEP for the benefit of students with disabilities in mainstream schools.

i. *Identify the children who required special education support.*
ii. *Conduct assessment to understand the nature of disabilities.*
iii. *Determine the suitable SPED programmes.*
iv. *Planning of suitable intervention by a multidisciplinary team of experts.*
v. *Preparation of IEP by the experts.*
vi. *IEP review meeting with relevant stakeholders.*
vii. *Accept inputs from parents and students and finalize the IEP.*
viii. *Implement the strategies as per the prepared IEP.*
ix. *Determine the progress evaluation and prepare review reports.*

x. *Identify the local resources for support services.*
xi. *Determine follow up services as required.*
xii. *Identify the best practices that can be practiced in schools.*
xiii. *Develop remedial plans for special education.*
xiv. *Preparation of local teaching and learning materials.*
xv. *Evaluation of progress.*
xvi. *Develop the follow up services after evaluation as required.*

Effective Management of IEP is explained as a separate chapter in this book for the benefits of the readers, teachers and rehabilitation practitioners.

3.5. Areas to highlight in an Effective Curriculum Management

The following components are very much significant in terms of curriculum management of children with special needs.

Knowledge:

All the children should have access at-least to grade level or more knowledge and skills as planned in the standard curriculum. A child with disability should also be enhanced with maximum possible practical learning experiences considering the nature of their disabilities. The children should not be discriminated from any learning experience. Appropriate strategies and technologies should be used to improve the learning environment. All the children with special needs should be provided with sufficient books and learning materials along with the curriculum transaction in schools.

Mental health

Mental health of the child is a key factor in learning. The intelligence level, span of attention, hyperactive behaviour, learning skills, physical and emotional conditions of the child etc. is to be considered in curriculum transaction. Experience shows that, it is not practical to provide the entire curriculum experience to children with disabilities due to various disorders of the child. S, the schools should take initiate to provide need-based curriculum focusing on the functional level of the child. Some substitutions may be required focusing on relevant subjects and components to boost the learning condition of the child.

Physical health

Physical health is an essential factor in improving learning condition. Children with limited mobility and physical disabilities cannot participate actively in many of the outdoor activities that are required for schooling. Such situations should be handled with the support of peers and siblings. Activities may be adapted considering the physical condition of the child. For example, a wheelchair bound child is not expected to participate in a soccer or cricket match like a non-disabled peer group. However, an efficient teacher can adapt some game for the group where the special child can also participate.

Social skills and manners

Social and behaviour skills development are the expected elements in a school education. Children with behavioural disorders may take a long time to develop such skills. Behaviour modification, developing acceptable manners, developing a positive attitude etc. are to be focused along with the regular curriculum. Service of a Counsellor or an Educational Psychologist is to be provided to children in case of a child with behaviour disorders in the mainstream classroom.

Behavior and emotional control

Experience shows that, children with attention deficit disorders (ADD), attention deficit hyperactive disorders (ADHD), low intelligence level or learning disabilities etc. are taking long time than the regular children to get desirable behaviour and emotional control in public schools. Such children may need firm handling, counselling, or behaviour therapy to get emotional development. Chances are evident for misbehaviors, bullying, hyperactivity, impulsivity, inattention, illegitimate behavioural tendency etc. it would be difficult to manage such children if the school fails to handle them effectively at the early stages itself.

Vocational skills

Pre-vocational and vocational skill development should be a part of IEP of children with special needs as many of the children are facing difficulty in finding their livelihood after their schooling or university studies. Since the middle school the child should get opportunities to develop basic skills and abilities to do some vocational training, so that the child can be enrolled for suitable job training courses after their studies in schools. The child's attitude, aptitude, functional academic skills, physical strength, intellectual level, behaviour level, safety etc. are some of the key facts needs to be considered when select vocational training for children with disabilities. Government and non-governmental agencies are conducting many training centers for vocational education in various parts of our country. It is a highlight that the people with disabilities are eligible to get certain percentage of job reservation as per the government norms. Hence, it is very much imperative to enhance the children with disabilities to focus on suitable vocational training along with their studies or soon after schooling.

Life skill education

Life skill education is considered as the acquisition of skill development required for everyday life after one's education. Acquiring life skills are the basic aim of education rather than learning the endless theories. The learner should be able to live independently in his society after his education. Hence, curriculum should focus on developing life skills so that the learner can be benefitted from his education. What is the benefit of education if one cannot develop such life skills even after 10 or 15 years of education in a school or university? Therefore, the foremost focus of education of a child with disability should be concentrated on skill development to face life with courage and confidence.

Skill development in the following areas is the basic prerequisite of every child with disability to be enrolled in education and employment like any other people.

- Physical Skills
- Emotional and Behavioural Skills
- Time Management
- Communication and Social Skills
- Motor Skills Development
- Problem Solving
- Critical Thinking
- Personal Hygiene and Appearance
- Responsibility and Integrity
- Positive Attitude and Adjustment Skills
- Continuing Education and Learning Skills in the Selected Vocational Avenues
- Aesthetic Skills
- Skills in Using Needful Technology

Learning and skill development are the basic components of any curriculum that is developed for an academic system. It is the right of the child to participate in regular school activities and co-curricular learning along with other children. However, it is noted that many of the children cannot follow all the curriculum activities as a result of personal constrains caused due to a disability or disorder. However, the child is expected to understand the basic curriculum. In case, if the child cannot follow the regular curriculum, a compensatory curriculum can be prescribed for such children.

The basic curriculum requirements in the compensatory curriculum are explained in this section.

3.6. Curriculum adaptation

It is observed that many of the children with disabilities are not able to follow the entire regular curriculum due to their physical, sensory, or emotional disorders. So, it is advised to follow an adapted curriculum considering the nature of disabilities the child is facing. For example, a child with blindness is not expected to learn to draw a picture based on the regular curriculum. A child with hearing impairment cannot follow a music class like their non-disabled peers. A child with physical disability is not expected to participate in an activity where a physical strength is required. So, all the learning and teaching experiences should be modified based on the functional level of the learner. Some elements from the regular curriculum may be modified or replaced with different activities considering the need and nature of the client.

Adaptation of curriculum is one of an important strategy for the education of children with special educational needs. In an inclusive classroom, all the children are expected to follow a grade level curriculum prescribed for a set of students considering their age and grade level. However, a child with disability may face difficulty to follow the regular curriculum along with other mainstream children. In this circumstance, needful adaptation is suggested to make the child to follow the prescribed curriculum. Some sort of modification, substitution, addition or deletion of curriculum may be considered to make the child to understand the concept considering the intelligence level, physical condition, sensory abilities, span of attention and behaviour level. For example, how to explain the concept of an elephant to a child with visual impairment? It is difficult to give the real concept in a classroom environment. A picture of an elephant is sufficient to make a regular child understand this concept. The child with visual disability needs modelling and more explanation than the other students. Similarly, a child with hearing impairment cannot follow the verbal explanation, music or a lecture in the classroom. Appropriate teaching strategies need to be followed to make the child understand the concept with the help of trained specialists to transact the curriculum for such children. The purpose of curriculum adaptation is to enhance the child's ability to understand maximum knowledge and concepts considering their functional skills and not to follow the entire pre-planned syllabus. It is always advisable to follow the functional curriculum that supports a special child in the future and makes them independent in life.

3.7. Functional Curriculum

Functional curriculum comprises of different modules as follows:

1. Academic - Reading, Writing, & Arithmetic (Three R's)

Basic skills in reading, writing and arithmetic are considered as the basic academic curriculum of school education. When talking about the primary skills the three R's (reading, writing & arithmetic) are the key elements, starting at early stages soon after early preparation. A child with disability is also expected to learn such academic skills at the early stages like his or her peer group. To achieve such skills the child should be enrolled in school at a right age like any other non-disabled child. Experience shows that many of the families are hesitant to send the child with disability to schools as most of them believe that the child cannot progress like other children. Due to delayed school enrolment the child with disability lacks the experience and may face difficulty to learn the skills and such delay may affect their learning skills and academic achievement. Hence, parents and teachers are advised to enhance the early identification, intervention, and school enrolment of children with disability at the early stages.

2. Daily living skills

All the children are expected to develop life skills for adaptive and positive behavior that enables them to be efficient and independent in school and daily living. Self-awareness, emotional management, positive behavior development, communication skills, decision making, creative thinking etc. are some of the life skills that a child is expected to develop at early stages. A child with disability may show delay in acquiring such skills due to various reasons.

Daily living skills are the compensatory skills that a child with disability needs to acquire at the early stages. Daily living skill development is the basic curriculum module for children with special educational needs. Due to the disability the child may show delay in developing daily living skills or some children cannot develop few of the essential skills. So, training in developing such skills should be considered along with the regular curriculum. Children learn the required life skills mostly in the primary classes. Due to the onset of disability many of the children cannot be enrolled in primary classes on time. Or they may take long time to achieve such skills. Thus, daily living skill development should be an essential component in the regular curriculum of children with special educational needs.

Following are the key skills to develop at the early stages:
- Sensory Training
- Concept Development
- Behavior Development
- Social Skills Development
- Physical Development
- Entertainment
- Time Management
- Pre-Vocational Skills
- Adaptive Skills
- Use Of Assistive Devices
- Independent Life Skills

Physical skills, Cognitive skills, Communication skills, Self-help or adaptive skills, preschool preparation, schooling & special education are some of the important aspects to be considered for the curriculum transaction of children with special needs.

3.8. Curriculum Evaluation

Evaluation is one of the major challenges in the education and rehabilitation of children with disabilities. When a mainstream child gets education in an education setting, the regular curriculum is the only component expected to be evaluated by the end of a semester or end of the year. However, a child with disability deserves multiple areas of evaluation, as such children are undergoing various medical, rehabilitation therapy and related support services. Along with regular academic, areas such as progress in physical growth, sensory development, therapy development, progress in mental health, intelligence level, span of attention, behaviour, vocational skills etc. are also to be evaluated. Overall, the evaluation of special children should be comprehensive focusing on the overall development of the child to make them independent in the society, as well as learn the pre-determined curriculum.

Following are some useful guidelines for practitioners for Preparation of Progress Report.

- Always appreciate the progress of the child even if it is a low-level achievement compared to other students in the classroom as the child is struggling with various disorders.
- Do not compare the progress with any other child as the achievement level varies for each student.
- Practitioners are advised to prepare separate evaluation/progress reports/ discharge report for each client.
- Long and short-term goal achievements need to be explained along with required follow up.
- Home schedule and follow up needs to be explained in the progress report.
- Needful tools and equipment names and methodology should be explained for follow up.
- Counselling and follow up of services if any should be specified in the report.
- Proper follow up and related institutions can be referred to the clients as required in case of higher level follow up.
- All the suggestions and recommendations need to be recorded in the school data system.
- These guidelines are for reference, and practitioners are advised to get proper guidance from the Department Heads/School Head for advanced and updated information if any.

3.9. Aspects of Successful Curriculum Planning

Following are the key aspects of successful curriculum planning and implementation in public schools:

1. Early assessment and availability of multidisciplinary clinical facilities
2. Reference to Specialist clinics as needed for medical services
3. Facilities for objective assessment
4. Expertise for the preparation of short- & long-term goals,
5. Strategies for implementation of effective Individual Education Plans
6. Availability of allied health and rehabilitation support services
7. Availability of assistive devices and technology
8. Explain home follow up to the parents as required
9. Effective involvement of teachers, parents and other stakeholders
10. Client education as and when needed
11. Effectiveness of counselling and follow up services
12. Home training programs as required
13. Quality management of support services
14. Effectiveness of re-evaluation over a period of planned IEP
15. Quality of reports and recommendations for follow up
16. Record of all the data using appropriate data information system

Selection of curriculum for children with special needs are depend on the following condition.

1. Available resources for supporting children with disabilities
2. Demand of the family and society
3. Age of onset of disabilities
4. Nature of disabilities
5. Intelligence and behaviour level of the child
6. Learning readiness of the child
7. The facilities available for teaching activities

8. Availability of special aids and appliances
9. Skills of specialists to offer services
10. Trained manpower in teaching and support services

3.10. Principles of curriculum transaction in inclusive schools

As explained earlier effective curriculum is the basic requisite of effective inclusive education of all children and effective IEP is the key tool for education of all in mainstream schools. The following principles need to be considered for effective curriculum transaction to enhance the equity and inclusion of all the students in public schools.

- Curriculum is the totality of experience, it does not mean only the academic experience that a student receives at school, but it should be the whole experience
- A planned curriculum gives the students an increasing awareness about the learning environment and prepares them for effective school life
- Curriculum should be planned to develop overall development of the student
- Curriculum should be adapted as and when needed to develop desirable changes of the learner along with other progress areas,
- Age, nature of disability, behaviour, intelligence, functional level etc. should be considered in curriculum transaction
- Ability, skills and interest of the learner needs to be considered
- Learning experiences should be designed to suit the interests and taste of the learner
- Consider the environment in which they live
- Teachers, parents, and students should know what is expected to be achieved from the school within the stipulated time.
- Equipment, tools, aids, activities, life situations etc. should be listed in the curriculum and the same should be shared to all stakeholders without restrictions to provide equal opportunities

Evaluation should be the part of every step of curriculum development to prepare the children to face the challenges in education. The professionals are expected to have high skills in curriculum planning so that the education and rehabilitation will be effective for the independence of children with special educational needs.

"The highest result of education is tolerance."

Helen Keller

*****

Section: 4

Effective IEP for Academic Challenges
A Practical Approach for Successful Inclusion

Section: 4

Effective IEP for Academic Challenges
A Practical Approach for Successful Inclusion

Units:

4.1. Different Categories of Children with Special Needs

4.2. Objectives of a Structured Individual Education Plan

4.3. What is an Individualized Education Plan (IEP)

4.5. SMART Goals

4.6. Owner of IEP.

4.7. Guidelines for Practitioners for Effective IEP Preparation

4.8. Rehabilitation support services

4.9. Suggested Activities in Rehabilitation for Effective IEP

Section: 4

Effective IEP for Academic Challenges
A Practical Approach for Successful Inclusion

'Special Education' is a broad term used to describe the educational system of children with Special Educational Needs (SEN). SEN refers to children with physical, sensory, psychological, or behavioral disorders or disabilities. Different research studies indicates that 5-7% of the children in our public educational system are facing some sort of disorders that obstructs the effortless education and learning process of the child. Such group of children need some special support and care in education and daily life along with regular school activities. To develop their maximum possible capability, such special children, need specialized instructions, counselling, or support services according to their peculiar needs and nature of the problems. These specialized support service programmes or instruction strategies are known as special education. In olden days special schools were considered as a place of special education for all the categories of children with disabilities.

It does not mean that these children need only special schools, or a specialized center for rehabilitation, but the strategies and child-centered education are the key factors in educating these children. Support Services Centers and preschools can play a vital role in education and mainstreaming of such children. As per educational psychologist's, Special Education should be based on a structured Individualized Education Plan (IEP).

Individualized Education Plan consists of a child-centered curriculum, appropriate rehabilitation therapy support services and participation of school, home, and community in the process of education. Like any other, a child with disability must also be enrolled in a formal education programme at an early stage so that the child can be prepared well and can address the unique educational needs considering their peculiar nature of disability.

As per the Individuals with Disabilities Education Act (IDEA) passed in 1975 in the United States, concerned educational institutions are expected to provide special education and related support services to all the eligible students. The eligibility of special education support is based on the classification of disabilities in the disabilities act in every country. As per IDEA, special education should be planned individually for the overall development of the child with a disability or special needs especially, self-help skills, communication, literacy and numeracy, physical skills, vocational skills and prepare them for their success in the present and future life.

4.1. Different Categories of Children with Special Needs

As per the Right of Person with Disabilities Act (2016), passed in Indian Parliament, 21 categories are considered as disabilities, who need special care and support in society. They are as follows:

i. Blindness
ii. Low Vision
iii. Leprosy Cured persons
iv. Locomotor Disability
v. Dwarfism
vi. Intellectual Disability
vii. Mental Illness
viii. Cerebral Palsy
ix. Specific Learning Disabilities
x. Speech and Language Disability
xi. Hearing Impairment (Deaf and Hard of Hearing)
xii. Muscular Dystrophy
xiii. Acid Attack Victim
xiv. Parkinson's Disease
xv. Multiple Sclerosis
xvi. Thalassemia
xvii. Hemophilia
xviii. Sickle Cell Disease
xix. Autism Spectrum Disorder
xx. Chronic Neurological Conditions

xxi. *Multiple Disabilities including Deaf Blindness*

All of the above group of children need different types of education, rehabilitation and support services for their education and independent life along with their peer group and siblings.

4.2. Objectives of a Structured Individual Education Plan:

The development of Individual Education Plan (IEP) is a fundamental step in the promotion of special education of students identified as having any physical, sensory or behavior disorders or disabilities. Special education program focuses to accommodate all the children with special educational needs or children with disabilities to get the most suitable education and learning services considering the unique nature of disorders. Following are the key objectives of any special education program for the development of children with special needs:

1. To identify the unique nature and intensity of disorders
2. To identify the strength, weakness and unique educational needs considering the nature of disabilities or disorders
3. To determine the required special education services for each child with disability
4. Early preparation of special children for special education
5. Develop the required individual education plan
6. Develop or adapt curriculum required for the child considering their need and nature
7. Selection and introduction of appropriate assistive devices for special education
8. Coordination of parents, teachers, and peer group for curriculum transaction
9. To guide the parents, teachers, or child to develop skills and abilities of the child
10. To determine the appropriate model of special education for the child
11. Select the suitable models of educational programs

12. Development of daily living skills in children with disability
13. Evaluation of special education services whenever require
14. Modify the IEP as and when required based on the student progress
15. Determine the role of specialist staff
16. Preparation of tips for the safety and security of special children
17. Arrangements of volunteers'/teacher aides or family members for support
18. Develop communication plan for those who are involved in the process of special education
19. Conduct review meeting with parents and school authorities

With all the above aims, our public educational system is expected to accept the above children in the mainstream education as a part and parcel of education and learning services along with their peer and siblings. This concept is called Inclusive Education.

Inclusive Education is a process of accommodating all students in the neighboring schools in age appropriate, mainstream classes and with necessary support services. Inclusive education provides equal educational opportunities to all the children without any discrimination. Inclusion aims at the protection of a child's right and full participation in school and community activities. Proper Individualized Education Plan (IEP) is the key aspect of a special education program, whether it is a specialized school or a regular mainstream school system.

As per the new National Education Policy 2020 (NEP 2020, India), in a mainstream inclusive school, all children are equally accepted irrespective of color, class, creed, or disability. The Right of Persons with Disabilities Act 2016, states that it is the responsibility of every educational institution to enroll the children with special needs in the public education system without discrimination and provide them education and opportunities for sports and other recreation activities equally with others. (Mithu Alur & Tony Booth).

4.3. What is an Individualized Education Plan (IEP)?

IEP is a 'smart written document' developed for each individual child with special needs which specifies the special education needs, with achievable goals, adapted curriculum considering the strength and weakness of the child, required support services, required tools and equipment and all related items for progress during a specific period. Graham Clunies Rose (1983) explains that each handicapped child must be provided with a written individualized education plan (IEP), which states what educational services will be provided to the child. The IEP is considered as an essential document for the development of skill development considering the unique nature of disabilities. All the advanced countries agree the need of IEP for the overall development of children with special educational needs and their special education program in public or private education system. Modern Educational psychologists' emphasis the important of 'Smart IEP' for effective inclusion of children with special needs in the mainstream schools.

Aim of a smart IEP.

A SMART Goal or and effective IEP aims to offer a systematic education and development plan for a child with disability. Following are the other key objectives of an effective IEP:

- Ensuring the key need and nature of special educational needs considering the disability condition
- Assuring the right of the child and parents to receive appropriate care and special education as per the nature of disability
- Determining the therapeutic and related support services required to enhance the child to be independent along with his/her peer group
- Determine the extracurricular, co-curricular, daily living skills development plans for further development

- Explain the needful curriculum adaptation as required for the child with disability
- Determining the educational requirement considering the various functional level of the child
- Identifying the needful tools and equipment required to educate the child as per the curriculum transaction
- Determining the required skills in communication, social interaction, entertainment, sensory development, adapted physical activities, pre-vocational skills and required areas
- Determining the quality and quantity of educational needs and services and support each student individually to attain the goals
- Ensure that students with disabilities receive required teaching strategies and support, and protect the rights of disabled students regulated within policy and culture
- Determining the curriculum components that can be included in the virtual education program

Ideally, an effective IEP must be approved by the parents and school authority who knows much about the need and nature of the child with a disability. The specialized professionals are legally responsible for providing the services described in the IEP. So, to achieve the objectives of a Special Education Program, IEP is awfully important and essential for a structured set up. IEP in other words can be interpreted as smart goals. The quality of a smart goal prepared for the special education will reflect the quality of the entire education and rehabilitation support services.

All the special education professionals and practitioners in support services system have to be instructed to follow a standard SMART plan. A professional approach should be followed in IEP preparation, evaluation and progress reports preparation of all the clients. This method is effective for helping practitioners to set goals that are aligned with high-quality services to equip children with disabilities like any other children in the society.

4.5. SMART Goals

The idea of S.M.A.R.T. goals developed in the beginning of 1980, and it became the most accepted tool and methodology in effective goal attainments in special education and rehabilitation support services. It is a tool to create criteria to help improve the chances of succeeding in accomplishing a goal. These methods were found to be useful for the planning and preparation of special education support service programs too. This section explains about the smart goals and its relevancy in special education support services for an effective inclusive education program for children with disabilities and special educational needs.

The acronym stands for:

I. **S – Specific**

When setting an individual education plan for a child with special educational needs, be specific about what you want to achieve in a specific period. The plan should be prepared considering the physical condition, sensory level, cognitive condition, functional academic level, psychological condition, behavior, and the span of attention. Think about this as the mission statement for your child's specific achievement over a period of time. The plan should include an answer to the popular 'W' questions to make it specific.

- *Who* – Consider who needs to be involved to prepare the individual education plan for the child and achieve the goal. This is essential when you are working for a group of children with disabilities in their special education program.

- *What* – The educator is expected to plan exactly what they are trying to achieve. Make sure, what are the expectation of a practitioner and parent about the achievement of the child. For example, considering the nature of disabilities what are the new components the child is going to achieve from the age level curriculum, adapted areas of curriculum, new concepts etc. The practitioner should be always answerable to the question "What are you going to achieve with your plan?". The progress report should reflect the answer of achievement throughout the plan period.

- **When** – All the children with special needs cannot achieve all the goals in the stipulated common time frame. So, tutors should be able to set a time frame to achieve the prepared goal considering the strength and weakness of the child, which means the plan should be "time-bound" and should be achievable in time. Short term or long-term goals should be specified in the plan so that the tutor and parents can focus on both areas separately considering the functional level of the child.

- **Where** – The location of the child is very much important while you plan an IEP. Special child may be enrolled in a special school, inclusive school, or a part time support service center to avail required services. Or the child may be living at home or a school hostel setting. So, when select the components in the IEP, the location of the child needs to be considered. For example, some activities given in the plan may not be practical in a home setting. If the parents are not educated or supportive, the child may not be able to complete a task at home as planned. So, the location of the child must be considered in IEP planning.

- **Which** – It refers to the suitability of the selected component in IEP. Which component is beneficial for a particular period considering the need and limitation of the child? All the items should link with the previous experience and knowledge of the child. A methodology of 'Known to Unknown' to be followed when you select a smart goal for a child with disability. It will help the child to understand the concept well by linking the previous knowledge with the new concept.

- o *Why* – As an Educator, you are answerable, why you selected a particular goal for the child in the IEP. The SMART goal should be based on the requirement of the peculiar nature of disability. Consider the nature of disability, age of onset of disability, physical and other condition or the skills and abilities in learning, so, be the tutor.

- o Should be able to explain why a particular goal is selected. Keep in mind that the IEP should benefit the child for a long-term progress.

II.   M – Measurable

Which scale you are going to use to evaluate the functional skills of the child with special educational needs. When you prepare an IEP, make sure that it is measurable, and you are able to make progress reporting.   Both short- and long-term goals should be measurable. Considering the nature of disabilities, the Tutor should be able to evaluate all the areas including, academics, functional life skills, behavior and the use of tools and equipment if any in terms of a particular disability. The following points to be taken care in terms of evaluation of IEP.

- o Develop needful strategies for evaluation.
- o Evaluate short term and long-term goals separately.
- o Consider the peculiar nature of disability, age, and functional level of the child to achieve specific task.
- o Explain the achievement against the expectation of SMART GOAL
- o Consider the achievement level that help the child in the future daily living.

- Enhance the child for a self-evaluation of the IEP progress.
- Enhance the student and parents to understand the whole evaluation process by explaining the purpose and methodology of evaluation.
- Enhance the student and parent about the strength, weakness, and scope of opportunities through comprehensive evaluation to understand the real progress of the child.
- Highlight and appreciate all the areas of achievement as a motivation for further efforts.
- Follow up and guidance to the parents and child to achieve the progress at the home settings.

III.   A – Achievable

This determines the skill of the trainer to select the achievable smart goals for the child. Priority plays a vital role to select achievable goals. All the children doesn't need all the goals as the need and nature of disability and physical condition are varies from child to child. This focuses on how important a goal is to the child and what you can do to make it attainable and may require developing new skills. The goal should be to inspire the child to achieve and not for discouragement. Plan carefully how to accomplish the goal, how the set goals are useful for the child, what are the tools and equipment needed, and the strategies to educate the concepts depicted in the smart plan. A self-analysis is required to make sure that the goals prepared are achievable for the child concerned, based on the skill and limitation of the child. A smart IEP appreciates achievable goals.

IV.   R – Relevant

A smart goal should be relevant to address the educational and therapeutic needs of children with special needs. Relevance varies child to child as the physical and cognitive condition differs. A goal set for a child with a visual impairment is not applicable for a child with hearing impairment. Because the sensory level of both the children are different. Thus, each goal expected for each child should be based on the unique nature of the child and it should be in alignment with the overall progress of the client. For example, if the goal is to launch a rehabilitation component of a client, the goals should relevantly consider the nature of disability if any, intellectual level, sensory condition, functional level of the client, learning condition, interest of learning, family background, and easily adaptable to the client and parents as much as possible. Irrelevant goals will not help the child to improve and attain the goal of special education and rehabilitation support services in a mainstream school.

V.   T – Time-Bound

A time bound methodology should be followed to set a smart goal as there is an evaluation after the achievement of goals in a specific period. Short term and long-term goals should be specifically mentioned separately in the plan. Ask yourself about how much time you required to complete a task and what can be accomplished within that time. A mid-term evaluation is always suggested to make sure that you are on time to complete the targeted goals.

4.6. Owner of IEP.

Considering the best available standard of practices, a well experienced Special educator is expected to be the owner of an effective IEP planning in special education support service program. However, a group of IEP team members are also expected to be as a part of IEP preparation. Following professionals are important to contribute with their technical inputs to draft the effective IEP for children with special educational needs.

- Different Subject Teachers in Special Education
- Occupational Therapist
- Speech Therapist
- Physiotherapist
- Psychologist
- Behavior Therapist
- Training Specialist
- Pre-Vocational training specialist
- Other specialists in therapy or support services

Parent and the client also should be involved in every stage as a contributing member of an effective IEP.

4.7. Guidelines for Practitioners for Effective IEP Preparation

- An IEP is a road map for instruction and the essence of the special education process (Johns et al., 2007), which ensures the provision of the necessary services for a quality education and a successful school experience for all students with disabilities.
- Specialists are advised to prepare separate IEP for each individual student considering the need, nature, strength, and weakness of the client.
- Short- and long-term plan should be prepared and explained well in the IEP.
- Education and Therapy session components, home schedule, follow up instructions etc. needs to be explained in the plan.
- Needful tools and equipment required are also to be specified in the plan.
- Counselling details and follow ups needs to be explained in the plan.
- A standard model of IEP is to be followed by all the specialist in the same organization.
- Proper follow up is suggested in a stipulated time frame.
- Proper review should be carried out on time to time.
- IEP Team members should have thorough knowledge about the curriculum, skill development and the basic requirement of all the categories of children with special educational needs and disabilities.
- Individual differences, ability to follow teaching strategies and of the learning environment should be taken care in effective IEP preparation.

Essentials of IEP

Individual Education plan is consists of all the developmental activities that helps the child to get overall development considering the need and nature of disability. Obviously, academic development is the key component of the plan, however there are many more areas also needs to be considered in planning for over a period of time focusing short and long term development of the child focusing the nature of disability or disorders the child is struggling from. At the early stages of education proper early preparation is an essential component in IEP. Similarly, rehabilitation support services also considered as an indispensable factor in the process of individual education plan.

4.8. Rehabilitation support services

Rehabilitation support service is a compensatory service that enables the child to overcome the disability or disorders the child is facing at the early stages of development. For example, if a child is unable to speak at the early stages, speech therapy is a crucial service to be offered at the early stages of milestone development. Likewise, many more services are mandatory to make the child independent for learning and development.

Following are the key support services that need to be developed for rehabilitation support services for the overall development of children with various types of disorders.

- *Speech and language therapy*
- *Physical Therapy*
- *Occupational Therapy*
- *Psychotherapy*
- *Psychiatric therapy*
- *Applied behaviour analysis*
- *Hydrotherapy*
- *Art Therapy*
- *Food and clinical nutrition services*

- *Hippo therapy*
- *Training in Assistive devices*
- *Mobility training*
- *Sensory training*
- *Concept development*
- *Auditory training*
- *Pre-Vocational Training*
- *Counselling services*
- *Medical support services etc.*

Proper components from the above areas needs to be included in the individual education plan of all the children with special needs based on the assessment of multidisciplinary team of experts and considering the physical and functional level of each child separately. A skillful specialist plays a vital role in developing suitable individual plan for the benefit of each child with special needs separately. Coordination of professionals is highly suggested for effective individual planning and management of IEP to achieve effective equity and inclusion of all the children in mainstream public education system.

Following are the key features of a rehabilitation curriculum in a standard IEP

a. **Functional curriculum:** Most of the children with disabilities cannot follow the entire curriculum. So, it is always advisable to follow a functional curriculum considering the abilities, skills, nature of disorders, intellectual and functional level of the child.

b. **Compensatory curriculum:** Many of the areas of the general curriculum cannot be transacted to different categories of disabilities. Therefore, a need based compensatory curriculum is recommended for the education of children struggling with disabilities.

c. **Adapted curriculum:** Curriculum adaptation with modification, additions, deletion etc. are required for the easy transaction in classroom situation. A trained specialist service is always suggested to adapt the curriculum based on the functional level of the child with disability.

d. **Use of special aids and appliances:** Children with special needs are in need of various kinds of special aids and appliances than mainstream children considering the nature of disability. Such children should be well trained in using such tools for effective learning. For example, a child with visual impairment may be is in need of some special tools or assistive devices such as braille, abacus, tailors frame, mobility equipment, audio equipments etc.

e. **Preparation for life:** Life centered education is yet another key feature of education of special children. Many of the content in the curriculum may not be practically useful for such children. So, the teacher should focus to select life centered topics for the benefit of children focusing on long term development.

f. **Life skills education:** Life skills are essential components for the child to face life with courage and confidence. All the skills required for everyday life should be added along with an individual plan for the child with disability.

g. **Independency:** Curriculum planning should focus on making the child independent after schooling. The purpose of any curriculum is skill development for a suitable vocational training. Technical skills, communication, social interaction etc. are the key areas to focus on making the child independent.

h. **Daily living skills:** Skills in daily living such as personal hygiene, toileting, grooming, eating, dressing, manners, money handling etc. are highly essential to learn as a part of curriculum. High priority should be given to all such areas in the planning of IEP.

i. ***Curriculum evaluation:*** Continues and comprehensive evaluation is always required as part of quality individual education program. Experts from multidisciplinary team should be with the teachers and special educators to evaluate the long term and short-term progress of the child based on the given IEP. Follow up and parents counselling should be mandatory for the effectiveness of evaluation and further home training activities.

4.9. Suggested Activities in Rehabilitation for Effective IEP

Some of the common activities are given below as the sample for reference to prepare effective individual plan. Teachers and rehabilitation practitioners are expected to select such suitable activities for the long term and short-term planning of IEP.

Common components in rehabilitation – PT & Speech

Physiotherapy items	Speech Therapy
o Posture and positioning o Body alignment o Functional use of hands o Stable postural base o Body Balance o Range of Motion (ROM) o Any deformities affecting use of the extremities o Enhancement of Motor Experiences o Equilibrium and protective reactions o Muscle tone o Motor planning o Integration of muscles o Tactile input o Visual input	o Improve Eye contact o Attention improvement o Behavior modification o Responds to environment sounds o understand simple instructions o Follows simple commands o Understand Expressive language o Understand receptive language o Pointing skills o Correction of misarticulations o Vocabulary development

o Auditory input o Proprioceptive input o Kinesthetic input o Vestibular input o Bilateral coordination	o Understand the non-verbal clues o phrases o Simple sentences o Improve the rate of speech o Articulation corrections o Voice improvement o Oral pressure o Describe events o Comprehension o Proper vocabulary

Common components in rehabilitation curriculum – OT & SPED

Occ. Therapy	Special Education (Primary level)
o *Bilateral Coordination* o *Fine Motor Control* o *Tactile discrimination* o *Crossing the Midline* o *Upper Body Strength and Stability* o *Visual Motor Skills* o *Visual Perception* o *Dressing and undressing* o *Self-Care* o *Improving mobility.* o *Managing pain.* o *Self-care and independence.* o *Maximizing quality of life* o *Eating habits* o *Personal Hygiene* o *Dressing/clothing decisions* o *Upper Body Strength and Stability*	o *Reading* o *Writing* o *Arithmetic* o *Coloring* o *Concept development* o *Use of special tools* o *Use of assistive technology* o *Calendar* o *Time* o *Sensory Training* o *Daily Living Skills* o *Adapted physical activities* o *Functional curriculum* o *Adjustment* o *Communication skills* o *Socialization* o *Study skills*

Common Components in Rehabilitation Curriculum–Behaviour/ Daily Living

Behavior Development	Daily Life skills
o Developing Eye Contact o Fine & Gross Motor Development o Understand action words o Imitate oral motor movements o Follow instructions and commands o Body awareness o Understand communications o Identify people o Identify environmental objects o Identify environmental sounds o Understand dangerous objects o Identify desired objects o Understand social questions o Special relations o Understand the emotions of people o Seek help or give help as needed o Identify the labels o Understand social manners o Follow social orders o Behave well in public o Answer to social questions o Manners in using of public facilities o Understand social displays o Understand emergency contacts o Knowledge in social rules o Express the emotions	o Toilet training o Dressing/ Undressing o Personal Grooming o Cleanliness o Dusting/vacuuming o Washing o Folding/ washing/ironing o Use of protective objects (mask, sanitizer etc.) o Peel/cut fruits/vegetable o Eating habits o Making simple meals or juice o Use of money o Use of mobile phone, ATM cards etc. o Skills to Deal with transport facilities o Social interaction o Identify the needful locations o Identify personal relations o Arranging study room/ dining o Setting of personal belongings o Setting of room/ cupboards o Any other skills as required o Identify food items o Recognize dangerous objects

Effective IEP is the basic tool for the planning and management of a qualitative special education support service program. All the related professionals should work hand in hand for the preparation and implementation of IEP for creating an effective inclusive education and equity of children with special educational needs.

*****

"Don't struggle about the struggle. In other words, life's full of ups and downs. So if you're struggling, don't worry, everyone else has or will at some point."

– Sean Covey, writer

Section: 5
Challenging the Psychological Disorders

Section: 5
Challenging the Psychological Disorders

Units:

5.1. Common psychological challenges in inclusive schools

5.2. Challenging Psychological Disorders in School System

5.3. Other Challenging Disorders

5.4. Intervention to face the Psychological Challenges

Section: 5
Challenging the psychological disorders

Psychology is considered as the science of human mind and behaviour. Human mind is always found to be mysterious always and it is challenging to predict how mind is processing the thoughts and how people behave differently in various settings. Hereditary, environment and life circumstances play a critical role in molding the mind and behaviour of a person. All such factors determine the process of thoughts and reaction of people in the surrounding. A balanced mind and controlled behaviour are as important as a healthy body. So, study on human mind and behaviour are as equal as human health science. Therefore, this chapter discusses about human psychology focusing on the psychology of children and adolescents in the public education system. Various types of crucial psychological disorders, aspects related to the affected children, intervention methodologies, and related components in the management of psychological disorders etc. are discussed in this section by focusing the parents, teachers and related professionals dealing with children and adults with various psychological disorders.

When you deal with a suspected case, what impact you can bring to a child:

- o *You hug a child with a smile and express real love and affection.*
- o *You give a supporting hand to a sick person.*
- o *Appreciate a child when he achieves something new.*
- o *Visit a person who is hospitalized.*
- o *Visit a friend during his bad time.*
- o *Visit a person who is in a critical condition.*
- o *Support a mother when she is in trouble.*
- o *Being with child who failed in his examination.*
- o *Appreciate the child when he/she get a high achievement.*

All human beings are in need of some emotional support to live a peaceful life. Such emotional support boosts the mental health of a person and makes them feel happy, mentally healthy, and develop a feeling of safe and security in society where they live. So, psychological support is very much essential to all the individuals living in the society if they are found to be any behaviour, psychological or adjustment issues. Psychological support is required for positive impacts in all stages of human life since the onset of birth to the end of life to make them strong and stable and continue a balanced life. We pat or soothe a child when he cries. What effect we make through this act…? We sit with an aged and unhealthy person and speak for a few minutes. What effect does it have on him…? Experience shows that an open communication and establishing the feeling of security can bring huge changes in people who are suffering with psychological disorders. Once they feel that they have someone with them to support, someone to listen to their problems, most of the crisis can be resolved. Most of such issues can be solved by giving proper guidance, counselling or through minor intervention strategies.

There are various types of psychological challenges faced by the students in our stressful environment. It is estimated that 5% - 10% of children are having disorders such as disability, behaviour, psychological, emotional, or learning disorders. It is the responsibility of every school system to understand the common psychological and mental condition of the all the children and adolescence and provide counselling and intervention services in school and home settings to make them independent in society.

5.1. Common psychological challenges in inclusive schools

It is a known fact that there are various types of psychological disorders among children. Many such symptoms are overlapping and difficult to determine what exactly the problem is. The aspects explained in this chapter are not the symptoms of disabilities, but only considered as the variety of psychological conditions. Most of the countries had developed disability laws or disability support bills and classified disabilities and the provisions of possible services based on the guidelines of World Health Organization. Based on WHO guidelines India has also passed a disability act and 21 categories of disabilities are classified for educational and social benefits. But most psychological conditions are not covered by the Person with Disabilities Act in India. International Classification of Diseases (ICD) and the updated version of Diagnostic and Statistical Manual of Disorders (DSM- 5) are the globally accepted classification of mental disorders. DSM is the well accepted classification system in India; thus, this chapter explains the major categories of psychological disorders commonly found in our public school system. School teachers, counsellors or parents are expected to identify the disorders at the early stage and need to provide intervention services. A well-qualified and experienced school counsellor or a child psychologist can do needful intervention service at the early stages of onset of symptoms of disorders. However, they are not expected to give treatment if they are not qualified to provide medical services. The clients should be referred to a psychiatric or other related medical specialists for needful treatment and consultancy as needed.

5.2. Challenging Psychological Disorders in School System

As per the Diagnostic and Statistical Manual of Disorders (DSM- 5), there are about 300 types of disorders that are identified so far, and classified for support services. This chapter discussed about the prominent type of disorders. The professionals are expected to understand more about each disorder in case you are dealing with any symptoms in classroom or home setting of children and adolescence. Immediate intervention and referral services are the key responsibility of primary professionals dealing with clients and their parents, who are found to be suffering with the symptoms of psychological disorders.

The major psychological conditions classified in DSM-5 are as follows. Some of the symptoms explained below are overlapping with many disorders. So, assessment of a highly skilled specialist is always suggested to all the group of disorders before starting any treatment.

1) Neurodevelopmental disorders

Neurological disorders refer to the conditions of children those who affected with brain dysfunction and reflected in their speech, motor skills, posture, gait, poor daily living skills and other physical dysfunction. Cerebral palsy is a common example of Neurological disorders present in children. Motor coordination issues, mobility disorders etc. are some of the noted conditions in such children.

2) Neurocognitive disorders

Neuro cognitive disorders refers to the cognition or intelligence. Poor intelligence dysfunction in memory, retention, learning skills, learning disorders, dyslexia, dysgraphia, aphasia, attention deficit disorders, hyperactivity, impulsive behaviour, conduct disorders, epilepsy, language disorders, Alzheimer's, and dementia (inability to remember, think) etc. are the common features.

3) Sleep / wakeup disorders

Sleep disorder is the condition where the affected client cannot sleep or wake up as a normal child. Restless sleep, no-sleep, poor living skills, poor eating habits, poor academic skills, anger, difficulty in decision making, poor physical performance, unexpected accidents, poor reactions to dangerous objects, inability to understand the consequences etc. are the common nature of sleep disorders.

4) Anxiety disorders

Anxiety disorders are considered as the most common psychological conditions that affects major number of children and adults. Restless behaviour, fatigue, poor concentration, fear, easily irritable, poor muscle tone, difficulty to control the behaviour, sleep dysfunction, restlessness, presence of some phobias, like to be away from others, impulsive response, etc. are the common symptoms in such children.

5) Depressive disorders

Depression is a common mood dysfunction with persistent feeling of sadness and hopelessness. Such clients are poor or not interested in any daily activities or studies. Chronic body pain, digestive issues, isolated behaviour, absence of pleasure habits, significant weight loss, reduction of physical movements, lack of energy, laziness, inability to think or concentrate, repeated thoughts of death, frequent suicidal tendency, or a specific plan to commit suicide etc. are the common features of such children.

6) Bipolar and related disorders

American Psychiatric Association defines bipolar disorders as a group of brain disorders that cause extreme fluctuation in a person's mood, energy level and ability to function. Such children mostly experience over excitement, over activity, delusions, some manias, fluctuation of behaviour in extreme high or low, depression, unpredicted self-esteem, psychotic symptoms, extreme sadness, guilt, worthlessness, racing thoughts and speech over activity, enthusiastic, over happiness, suicidal tendency, decreased sleep, easily distracted, psychomotor agitation etc.

7) Schizophrenia spectrum and other psychotic disorders

Schizophrenia is a psychological disorder that occurs irrespective of any age group. Different conditions such as 'Childhood Onset Schizophrenia', 'Early Onset Schizophrenia,' and 'Very Late Onset Schizophrenia' etc. are reported by the psychiatrists with complicated conditions. Depression, intellectual malfunction, bipolar, and autism spectrum are inter-related and many of its symptoms have similarities. Multiple symptoms may be present in some children. So, identifying the disorders at the early stage is the primary requisition for intervention. Genetic factor for Schizophrenia spectrum and other psychotic disorders are common, so timely intervention is highly required.

8) Trauma and stress related disorders

Childhood trauma and stress related disorders are common psychological conditions these days due to various environmental conditions. Post-Traumatic Stress Disorders (PTSD) is one among such conditions reported in school going children that is considered as a challenging psychological condition. Continuous sexual abuse, failures in exam, parental stress to study, frequent physical and mental abuse, ritualistic abuse, witnessing of criminal activities, witnessing of one parent being abused repeatedly, terrorist attack, war situation etc. are some of the common situations caused, due to such traumatic and stress related disorders.

9) Substance related and addictive disorders

Substance abuse is yet another challenge faced by school going students these days. Substance addiction includes the following:
- Alcoholism
- Use of stimulants such as meth (methamphetamine), Adderall, LSD (Lysergic acid diethylamide), etc.
- Benzodiazepines addiction such as Xanax, Valium, Klonopin, Ativan etc.
- Opioid addictions such as Heroine, Vicodin, morphine Addiction to Tylenol, Tyrosine, caffeine etc.

These drugs are reported as the crucial cause of addictive disorders among school going children and young adults. Children addicted to such drugs may have an overdose leading to death in the worst case. Other complications that commonly occur are tachycardia, hypertension, anorexia, insomnia, depression and seizures. Suicidal tendency, paranoia, attention deficit, isolation, hyperactivity, criminal tendency, family destruction, mental illness, deprivation, etc. are some of the consequences of such drug abusive disorders.

10) Personality disorders

Personality disorders are a challenging issue among school going children these days. It was reported that many children, especially teenagers with personality disorders make troublesome situations in the mainstream school system. Problems such as bullying, self-injury, suicidal tendency, addiction, depression, antisocial activities, hyperactivity and aggressive behaviours are the common results causes from this condition. Personality disorders are grouped in different clusters as follows:

Cluster: A
- Paranoid personality disorder
- Schizotypal personality disorder
- Schizoid personality disorder

Social isolation, thinking disorders, inappropriate behaviours, poor or no social interaction etc. are the key features of such disorders.

Cluster: B
- Borderline personality disorder
- Anti-social disorders
- Histrionic personality disorder
- Narcissistic personality disorder

Impulsive nature, over emotions, unpredictable thinking, frequent emotional disorders etc. are the common features of such personality.

Cluster: C
- Obsessive Compulsive Personality Disorders (OCPD)
- Avoidant personality Disorders
- Dependent personality Disorders
- Dependent Personality Disorders
- Hyperactive disorders
- Autism spectrum disorders

High level of anxiety is the significant feature of such children. The common symptoms may vary or resemble with other conditions. Proper assessment and follow up is required to diagnose and provide intervention to the affected children, since the beginning of the onset of issues.

11) Disruptive, impulse control and conduct disorders

As per the American Psychiatric Association, disruptive, impulse control and conduct disorders are a group of disorders that are linked to varying difficulties in controlling aggressive behaviours, self-control, and impulsive behaviour. Such behaviours are threat to others in school. Fighting, disobedience, destroying property, stealing of various objects, breaking the norms and rules are the common behaviours reported. Such behavioural disorders are tend to be more common in boys than in girls. Intermittent explosive disorder, oppositional defiant disorder, conduct disorder, Kleptomania, other specified disruptive, impulse-control and conduct disorder, unspecified disruptive, impulse-control, etc. are the common disorders associated with disruptive, impulse control and conduct disorders

5.3. Other Challenging Disorders

There are numerous disorders found to be serious issues in school going children. Some of the most important disorders are as follows:

a. Somatic Symptom and Related Disorders
b. Feeding and eating disorders
c. Elimination disorders
d. Dissociative disorders
e. Sexual dysfunctions
f. Gender dysphoria
g. Paraphilia disorders
h. Disorders due to general medical conditions
i. AIDS related psychosis
j. Alcohol related psychosis etc.

In addition to the above behavioural issues, learning disorders such as dyslexia, dysgraphia, dyscalculia, Attention Deficit Hyperactivity Disorder (ADHD), etc. are also found to be the most challenging disorders in school settings. Depression and anxiety disorders are also noted as the key areas and that are mostly unattended in mainstream schools.

5.4. Intervention to face the Psychological Challenges

Coordinated efforts of the specialists and the support of multidisciplinary intervention is highly required for the betterment of affected children with psychological disorders. More than any treatment, emotional and mental support are the essential requirement of such children in the public school system. In addition to clinical intervention, following are the common support that can be given to such affected children.

- Be a good listener to the parent and the affected child with disorders
- Guidance and Counselling
- Refer to the clinical assessment and related support
- Create relation building and stress relieving situation
- Yoga and meditation
- Medication by psychiatrist / behaviour medicine specialist
- Resource mobilization
- Forgiveness exercise
- Yoga and meditation
- Education and therapy support
- Counselling Service
- Mental health professional support
- Follow up for all the required services

Practically, prevention and intervention are the accepted strategies in services of children affected with any psychological disorders. Every school should have an accepted intervention system in case if any child is affected with any such disorders. The first and foremost requirement in support of any disorder is to have a School Counsellor Service for initiating any intervention services. School system should have the facility to associate with experts from parents, clinical specialists or social workers to have expert opinion for any intervention services. The following are the key specialists who can offer support services in case if any child is found to be affected with any psychological disorders.

a. General Physician
b. Psychiatrist
c. Psychotherapist
d. Applied Behaviour Analyst (ABA Specialist)
e. Board Certified Behaviour Analyst (BCBA Certified Analyst)

    f.   Applied Child Psychologist
    g. Family Psychologist
    h. School Counselling Specialist

Mental health and well-being of all the children are equally important in our school system. It is the responsibility of our school system to ensure the identification of psychological disorders at the early stages and enhance the students and parents to get professional help to face and challenge the challenging situation in our school system.

*****

Mental Health:

"What mental health needs is more sunlight, more candor, and more unashamed conversation."
— *Glenn Close*

Equity:

"Equity in education is not just about providing equal resources, but also about addressing the unique barriers that some students face

-Unknown

Section: 6
Role of Professionals to Challenge the Challenges

Section: 6
Role of Professionals to Challenge the Challenges

Units:

6.1. School Psychologist

6.2. Speech & Language Pathologist (SLP)

6.3. Physiotherapist

6.4. Occupational Therapist

6.5. Behavioural Therapist

6.6. Audiologist

6.7. Optometrist

6.8. Assistive Technology Specialist

6.9. Recreational Therapist

6.10. Special Education Specialist

6.11. Clinical Management

6.12. Physiatrist / Primary Clinicians / Specialists

6.13. Case Manager / Social Worker

6.14. Parent's support group

6.15. Inclusion & Equity Management Team

Section: 6
Role of Professionals to Face the Challenges

Mother of a child is considered as the first dedicated specialist for child development and any other issues related to physical, sensory, psychological or behavioural disorders. The presence of parents gives a positive and safe environment to every individual. Parents can address most of the emotional and psychological issues with their children at the early stages as they are the most accessible and acceptable people for the children in their developmental stages. Once the children are enrolled in the schools, teachers are the most approachable person to address any such issues. A trained teacher with positive attitude can give required emotional support and guidance to the children, in case, if they require any such support. In addition to mother and teacher, a School Counsellor's support is also always advisable if a child faces any issues. Guidance and counselling are a part and parcel of the advanced educational system, and our public school system has always highlighted the need of such counselling system for all the children enrolled in schools. This chapter discusses about the role and responsibility of different professionals who are expected to provide support services to various categories of children in our public education system.

Coordination of Professionals

Coordinated efforts of parents and professionals are highly recommended for the overall development for the equity of inclusion of all the categories of children in our public education system. Following are the key professionals and key stakeholders who are expected to offer services for the education and skill development of children in an advanced society in addition to the regular teachers and administrators in our school system.

a. School Psychologist
b. Counsellor
c. Speech Language Pathologist
d. Occupational Therapist
e. Physical Therapist
f. Behavioural therapist
g. Audiologist
h. Special Education Specialist
i. Rehabilitation Operational Manager
j. Clinical Manager (Specialist)
k. Physiatrist
l. Primary Clinicians

Case Manager / Social worker
m. Case Management
n. Parent's organizations
o. Government agencies
p. Non-Government agencies

The role and responsibilities of important professionals are explained in the following paragraphs:

6.1. School Psychologist

School psychologist is one of the key professionals in the advanced education system. There are many branches of psychological services and experts who are supposed to help various groups of students facing varied mental health and psychological disorders in our mainstream education system. The key professionals in psychological services are categorized as follows. Below terms are used in different countries interchangeably.

- General Psychologist
- Clinical Psychologist
- Child Psychologist
- Educational Psychologist

- School Psychologist
- Counselling Psychologist
- Behaviour Psychologist
- Applied Behaviour Analyst
- Board Certified Behaviour Analyst (BCBA)

A qualified professional from the above areas is expected to serve as a school psychologist. In general, a School Psychologist is a qualified specialist in mental, social, behavioural and emotional development of children. Basically, two branches of psychologists deal with students with special needs during the school period. Typically, Child Psychologists deal with the developmental issues of children and Clinical Psychologists provide psychological evaluation and treatment for behavioural and emotional issues. Issues in genetics, personality, gender roles, cognitive development, sexual development, behavioural issues, adjustment problem, social growth and addressing the personality disorders etc. are some of the major topics of interest for the Psychologists.

A school psychologist is responsible to provide a wide range of services by helping the students to improve the mental health condition and boost the learning environment of children in school system. A skilled school Psychologist can also act as a School Counsellor who is responsible for the well-being and moral support of students in school. It's because of the psychological challenges, many of the students are unable to continue their education in a systematic way. Schools should be able to provide psychological support services since the early years, whenever they are identified as having some sort of difficulties. A school psychologist is expected to perform all the roles to strengthen the learning environment of the school system starting from Students and parents counselling. The following are some of the key responsibilities of the School Psychologist:

a. Psychoeducational assessment by administering psychological and educational tests, conducting

observations and interviews, and gathering relevant information in the assessment of students experiencing learning and adjustment problems.
b. Consultation for students and parents
c. Crisis Interventions
d. Conduct motivational training for students and their parents
e. Intervention with the direct issues of students
f. Provide comprehensive reports in case of any client issues
g. Examination counselling
h. Support the school authorities to identify clients with ADD, ADHD, Autism and behavioural disorders.
i. Understand students' issues such as learning and personality disorders and solve them internally or refer for consultation as and when needed.
j. Assessment and treatment of children and adolescents with anxiety disorders
k. Assessment and treatment of children / adolescents with autism spectrum disorders, toileting problems / issues, etc.
l. Evaluation and management of the emotional and behavioural problems associated with chronic physical illness and adherence to medical regimens
m. Management of children with behavioural problems, sleep disorders, pseudo seizures, conversion disorders, and
n. Monitoring developmental and academic progress and helping with school re-entry after extended absences.

Management of children with serious disorders need more clinical expertise. If schools cannot provide such clinical services, the child should be referred to the higher-level clinical facilities for further intervention services. Following are the Different approach of psychological services needed for the clients in case of complicated issues.
- *Cognitive approach*
- *Behaviour approach*

- o *Humanistic approach*
- o *Psycho analysis*
- o *Nodding*
- o *Leaning*

6.2. Speech & Language Pathologist (SLP)

Speech Language Pathologist (SLP) is a primary level professional who is responsible to support the children in speech and language development. SLPs work with students exhibiting the full range of communication disorders, including those involving language, articulation (speech sound disorders), fluency, voice/resonance, and swallowing. Language and Speech Assessment, diagnosis, treatment, etc. are the key responsibility of the Speech Pathologist in school system. Furthermore, prevention of speech, language, cognitive, voice and swallowing disorders, correction of misarticulation, language development, one-on-one sounds / oral and written language skills to communicate at school, at home, and in every facet of life are also some of the key responsibilities of SLP.

To keep up-to-date changes in primary education and inclusive education, speech-language pathologist plays a vital role as follows:

i. Consulting with clients and understanding their speech delays or level of disorders, if any.
ii. Assess the cause and nature of speech problems, for example, congenital problems such as cleft palate or acquired disorders after stroke or injury.
iii. Develop short and long-term speech therapy plan for service.
iv. Deliver a suitable treatment programme, working on a one-to-one basis or in groups, to enable each of your child to improve as much as possible.
v. Review and revise the programme as appropriate.

vi. Advise care givers on implementing a treatment programme and train other professionals in therapy delivery.
vii. Monitor and evaluate your child's progress.
viii. Write confidential case notes and reports, as well as information for clients, care-givers, related personnel or professionals.
ix. Manage a caseload, while taking into account on priority basis, waiting lists, successful outcomes, referral and discharge of service users.
x. Work within a team to improve the effectiveness of service delivery.
xi. Conduct personal development reviews with colleagues.
xii. Support newly qualified speech and language therapy assistants.
xiii. Plan and deliver training sessions.
xiv. Undertake clinical audit.

6.3. Physiotherapist

Physiotherapy is one of the key allied health services in the spectrum of support services where many children are expected to get different services from assessment to total rehabilitation. The children with any type of physical disabilities are expected to get multiple services from a physiotherapist (PT) for their physical growth and development. Physiotherapists examine each client and develop a plan for treatment techniques to promote the ability to move, reduce pain, restore function, and prevent disability. In addition, PTs work with individuals to prevent the loss of mobility before it occurs by developing fitness - and wellness-oriented programs for healthier and more active lifestyles. The treatment of PTs consists of restoring, maintaining, and promoting not only optimal physical function, but also optimal wellness and fitness, and optimal quality of life as it relates to movement and health.

As primary health care providers, PTs also promote health and wellness as they implement a wide range of services for children from infancy through adolescence in collaboration with their families and other medical, educational, developmental, and rehabilitation specialists. Physical therapy promotes independence, increases participation, facilitates motor development and function, improves strength and endurance, enhances learning opportunities, and eases challenges with daily caregiving.

Key Responsibilities of a Physical Therapist is school system are as follows:

- Consulting with clients and understanding their physical condition and symptoms.
- Clients / parents counselling.
- Comprehensive assessment of the client.
- Preparation of short term and long-term therapy plan along with multi-disciplinary team.
- Offer physiotherapy services.
- Provide home plans for follow up at home.
- Monitor the progress and guide the home exercises.
- Evaluation
- Coordination with other specialists for fine / gross motor developments.
- Provide technology services, as and when required.

6.4. Occupational Therapist

Occupational therapy is a specialized area for intervention to develop, recover and maintain meaningful activities for the overall development of clients with disabilities. Occupational Therapists (OTs) help children to gain independence and function in their "occupation" or "life roles". For children, this refers to their ability to use their bodies to play and achieve developmental gross, fine motor skills, sensory motor skills, and visual motor skills that children need to function and socialize in their home, school, play and community environments. Those skills are essential for academic readiness and achievement in the older child. In the case of an injury or debilitating illness, a support service professional should focus on rehabilitating children, allowing them to return to their daily routines at their highest level of function. Key Responsibilities of Occupational Therapist are as follows:

i. Consulting with clients and understanding their physical condition and therapeutic needs.
ii. Development of therapeutic plan.
iii. Offer occupational therapy services.
iv. Provide home plans for follow up at home.
v. Monitor the progress and guide the home exercises.
vi. Evaluation of occupational development.
vii. Co-ordination with other specialists for motor skills and attention.

6.5. Behavioural Therapist

'Behavioural Therapy' is a psychological approach to treat the mental health and behavioural disorders of children and to train them to keep their normal behaviours, which are expected by the society. Applied Behaviour Analysis (ABA) and Cognitive Behaviour Therapy (CBT) are some of the common behavioural therapy approaches widely accepted in the behaviour management of children with behaviour and personality disorders. The behavioural therapy helps the client to reinforce the desirable behaviours and eradicate the non-desirable or mal-adaptive manners. Behaviour therapy is action based, considering the nature of skills and abilities of the client. Behavioural therapy techniques are focused on activity-based teaching strategies, which enhance learning improvement along with desirable behaviour achievement. On our public education system, behavioural therapists play a vital role to provide evaluation and management of a variety of developmental / behavioural problems, for clients with developmental delay, autism spectrum disorders, ADD and ADHD. Key responsibilities of a Behavioural Therapist are as follows:

- Behavioural therapist is responsible for effective services to develop desirable behaviours in children with behavioural disorders.
- Perform various functions, providing effective care to clients suffering from depression and other related illnesses.
- Create and apply new techniques in behavioural therapy programmes.
- Implement quality behavioural therapist functions to change a client's destructive behaviour.
- Identify the odd behaviours of children with ADD, ADHD, Autism spectrum disorders and develop intervention plan.
- Help treat client's mental illnesses like substance abuse, anxiety, aggressive behaviour and phobias.
- Provide behavioural therapist services to clinics, hospitals, communities and resident-based settings.
- Provide strong emotional support to clients during behavioural therapy.
- Modify and change behavioural disorders and aspects in children and adolescents.
- Create contacts and make interactions with doctors, clinicians and other behavioural therapists while treating problems related to behaviours.
- Facilitate lifestyle changes for clients with behavioural problems.
- Provide needful training to parents and care givers to support children in their home setting.

6.6. Audiologist

Audiologist is a rehabilitation professional, who specializes in the diagnosis of hearing disorder and hearing balance in children and adults. Audiologists possess comprehensive knowledge of the human auditory systems, and they have extensive training in sound reproduction, which is critical to the accurate fitting and adjustment of hearing-aids. In fact, Audiologist is not required for all the schools and hospitals; however, all the children should have access to the service of an Audiologist whenever they have any hearing disorder. Audiologists provide all diagnostic and audiology tests and prepare comprehensive reports for various stakeholders required for the education and health system. Key Responsibilities of an Audiologist are as follows:

 i. Perform all diagnostic and necessary audiological tests.
 ii. Provide comprehensive reports for various stakeholders within the support team.
 iii. Fitting, adjustment and maintenance of hearing aids.
 iv. Treatment for balance disorders and tinnitus (ringing in the ears).
 v. Hearing and speech rehabilitation programmes.
 vi. Timely follow-up screening.
 vii. Educate families and team members.
 viii. Early Hearing Detection and Intervention (EHDI) & Audiology for schools.
 ix. Provide on-going audiology management.

6.7. Optometrist

Optometrist are the primary level eye care professionals dealing with the evaluation of eyesight. A skilled optometrist is expected to detect functional vision, visual impairment, sign of injury, eye diseases, eye dysfunctions, and other condition associated with visual function. Optometrist record vision function and report to Ophthalmologist for further treatment and recommend for optometric corrections, health assessment, prescribe spectacles, or other corrective measures. Generally, optometrist is expected to work along with an Ophthalmologist in a clinical set up as it needs a lot of devices and technology that is not practical to set up in school health system. Thus, the students who need support of the

Ophthalmologist or Optometrist should have access to well-equipped hospitals or clinics with adequate facilities.

6.8. Assistive Technology Specialist

Assistive technology means any techniques, tools or devices that helps someone with an impairment, disability or disorders to increase, maintain, or to improve the functional capabilities for their learning, vocational skills and daily life. Effective technology equipment, tools and services are required mainly in the following areas:

- Early identification of impairment and disabilities.
- Intervention services.
- Effective medical support.
- Assistive devices for compensation the medical condition.
- Support aids for survival, movement, and sensory support.
- Devices for early preparation and daily living skills.
- Devices for special needs education.
- Therapy tools and equipments.
- Special equipment for education.
- Communication equipment.
- Advanced technology for effective life.
- Entertainment technology.
- Hardware and software.

For all the above areas need trained and skilled specialist for the operational management of such assistive technology. Assistive technology doesn't mean that it should be high-tech. Sometime a simple technical equipment can change the life of such people with disabilities and the specialist using assistive technology can change the life of the people in the most successful manner.

6.9. Recreational Therapist

Recreational Therapist is a professional who helps the children to remediate to improve the functional and independence level along with other children in the inclusive classrooms and provide variety of opportunity for socialization. A recreational therapist is a rare professional in Indian context. Recreational Therapists utilizes a wide range of intervention and techniques to improve the physical, cognitive, emotional, social, leisure and entertainment of children. A therapist is expected to works with the child, their family members, care givers, teachers and others related people to improvement of their health and mental condition. Also, assist the child to develop skills, abilities, knowledge and behaviour for daily living and community involvement.

6.10. Special Education Specialist

Special Education is a group of programmes and methodologies designed to address the educational requirements of children with unique educational needs. It includes different teaching strategies, needful plans, special tools, appliances and additionally it offers necessary support services. A Special Education specialist is a trained professional, who works with children having a variety of disabilities or learning disorders. Children with special needs require unique strategies from trained specialist to help them achieve their highest potential and to strive to progress beyond their limitations. Special educators work based on the Individual Education Plan (IEP), based on the unique educational needs and nature of disabilities. Based on the nature of disabilities the following are the common specialities of special educators serving in schools.

1. Special Educator – Visual Impairment/ Low Vision
2. Special Educator – Hearing Impairment
3. Special Educator – Deaf Blind
4. Special Educator – Learning / Intellectual Disabilities
5. Special Educator – Autism Spectrum Disorders
6. Special Educator – Sign Language Interpreter
7. Special Educator – Mobility Instructor

8. Special Educator – Braille Specialist

9. Special Educator – Assistive Technology

Experience shows that, for severe categories of disabilities, training in daily living skills and functional academics; use of special tools, appliances etc. are the essential components in special education; whereas mild to moderate group of disabilities need more of regular curriculum with necessary adaptation and they can be enrolled in public education system with minimum support services. Many children with special needs require some sort of curriculum modification with the support of special educators or regular teachers and such children are considered as the best example of successful integration in the public education system. Most of the special educators instruct students at the pre-school, primary or middle school levels and after they are being trained in early stage, mild to moderate level of disabilities may be continued in their education in public schools, with minimum support, or may be diverted to some vocational training programmes.

If specialized support areas such as Braille and special appliances for children with visual impairment, communication strategies for hearing impairment and deaf-blind, mobility training, behaviour analysis, rehabilitation therapy services, etc. are not required; such children can be easily integrated into public schools at early stages. If children are in need of such support services, every possible step should be taken to offer them support services at early stages of development so that such children can be educated at par with their peer group.

In addition to the above-explained specialists, the following groups of personnel are also needed to support the special children for their comprehensive rehabilitation and education.

10. Teacher Aide / Shadow Teacher

11. Volunteers
12. Community Workers
13. Nutrition Specialist
14. Mobility Instructor
15. Sign Language Specialist
16. Low Vision Specialist
17. Adapted Sports And Games Specialist
18. Orthotic And Prosthetic Specialist
19. Trained Nurse / Care Giver
20. Hydro Therapist
21. Hippo Therapist
22. Music Therapist
23. Vocational Instructor
24. Daily Living Skill Trainer Etc.

All the above personnel are expected to work with the child, their family members and other related personnel for the improvement of the child's health, education and behavioural development. Also, assist the child to develop skills, knowledge and behaviours for daily life and community involvement. The goals of such specialists are to restore, remediate or rehabilitate in order to improve the functioning and independence as well as to reduce or eliminate the effects of illness or disability.

6.11. Clinical Management

A clinical manager is responsible for overseeing the administrative operations of clinics and other technical facilities in a support service system. A qualified social worker or an accredited professional can be a good Clinical Manager. The role of a clinical manager is similar to that of a practicing administrator, which includes supervision and evaluation of service staff such as therapists, nurses and administrative employees. The Clinical Manager is responsible for ensuring clinical operations, clinical programme planning, implementation, monitoring and evaluation. The school supervisor can work together with the Case Manager to ensure the clinical issues related to each client, therapy services, equipment and client satisfaction. A regular mainstream school doesn't require a clinical manager; however, the clinical management is highly recommended for the operation of support service system at least in the district or block level support service system.

6.12. Physiatrist / Primary Clinicians / Specialists

A physiatrist is a medical practitioner who is supposed to be specialized in physical medicine and rehabilitation. The clients should have access to such specialists in a Center or a nearby hospital, so that, the client gets regular consultations if they have any issues with movement disorders, physical disability, cerebral palsy, pain, injuries, arthritis, tendonitis or spinal cord issues. The physiatrist may request to discuss the case with the therapist and evaluate the child to determine suitability of the referral. The physiatrist is also responsible to provide an updated status of the child's medical condition and needful recommendation for future treatment. The child may be referred back to the physiatrist by the therapist for review. A frequent consultation is required for the clients, if they have any sensory issues or associated disabilities.

The services of primary clinical practitioners are considered as general consultation. In addition to such general specialties, other specialty of medical services such as pediatric, ENT, Neurology etc. are also needed in service of such children as the referral services.

6.13. Case Manager / Social Worker

The case manager and / or social worker is responsible to ensure that families receive an orientation to the services, programmes and general guidelines related to the treatment process such as scheduling, equipment process and orders, treatment sessions, and their responsibility and rights. The Case Manager and / or Social Worker liaise between all members of the interdisciplinary team and the family. Such specialists are responsible to collect the relevant data and primary medical condition of each client and make it available for the specialists as and when required. The follow up, appointment, reports and follow up of services etc. are some of the key responsibilities of social worker. Needful primary information should be made available from social worker for the effective preparation of parents to accept the disability of the child at the screening stages.

A special education teacher can be an effective case manager in a special education support service programme. The Case Manager is responsible for making a schedule for clients and specialists based on availability of resources and the child's needs. The case manager will co-ordinate the delivery of special education services and will be the primary contact for the parent. Data collection, report preparation, discharge of services, etc. are some of the main roles of a Case Manager. Some of the other roles are as follows:

1. File reviews to monitor due process
2. Review of a student(s) special education file, evaluation reports, and any part of the IEP
3. Management of data and reports
4. Co-ordination with parents and schools
5. Plans weekly schedule for all support services
6. Ensuring plans and policies to parents and team members
7. Emergency contacts management

8. Manage health, safety and security
9. Incident and accident reporting
10. Conducting the IEP meeting
11. Dealing with demanding parents

Currently such a well-organized structure is not available in our public school system in India, but we need to develop an organized structure for the effective management of support services in our school system.

6.14. Parent's support group

In addition to all of the above specialist support services of the children with disabilities, parents play a vital role for the developmental process. The most important role of parents is to identify the specific issue of the child at the early stage and take him or her for needful medical treatment as and when needed. From assessment to total rehabilitation, various supports are expected from the parents as follows:

1. Provide needful early identification and medical intervention services at the early stage.
2. Identify the specialist clinics for proper diagnosis and provide needful medical support to the child.
3. Take appropriate steps to prevent disorders or disability at the early stages.
4. Make sure of the safety and security of the child.
5. Get an expert opinion, and if needed provide services such as physiotherapy, occupational therapy, speech and language therapy or special education services out of the school whenever required.
6. Provide suitable specialist support considering the disability.
7. Introduce the child to all walks of society and take them to social gatherings.
8. Develop a positive attitude towards the child with special needs and enhance others to develop desirable attitude towards such a child.

9. Enroll the child in an appropriate educational system considering his or her nature of disability, if any.
10. Make sure the attendance of the child in the school is regular.
11. Provide private tuitions, if the child faces any difficulty in any learning areas.
12. Communicate with the school and attend meetings with school authorities whenever required.
13. Support the child by following all the instructions given in IEP from the school.
14. Procure and provide assistive devices as per the child's needs.
15. Provide special transportation, if required.
16. Arrange assistants or guides, if required.
17. Participate in the assessment of the child and ensure that the child is to be felicitated appropriately by the principal or any other concerned authority.
18. Develop proper behaviour and discipline in the child with his or her peer group.
19. Support the child to get social benefits.
20. Provide needful vocational training whenever required.
21. Mobilize the community support for a community-based rehabilitation.
22. Provide opportunities for extra-curricular activities such as sports and games or any other form of entertainment.
23. Arrange local technological support whenever required.
24. Keep in touch with the visiting specialist, if any, in school or community.
25. Get medical or disability related certification for further use.
26. Act as an advocate for the child to engage him in social life, just like any other child in the society.
27. The parents of a child with special educational needs can provide valuable information to the school in relation to their child's learning difficulties, learning differences and learning preferences.

Participation of parents for early support is very important as it requires a lot of decision-making. The most important thing is to ensure that they are involved with and take an active role in programme planning and service delivery, based on an Individual Education Programme (IEP) team that determines a student's future.

6.15. Inclusion & Equity Management Team

Management and related stakeholders are equally responsible for the overall development of the inclusion and equity of children in a public education program. Project planning, development, implementation, evaluation, budgeting and quality improvement etc. are the various stage in successful education program. The management should have clear vision, mission and standard practices and procedures for the development of children in school system. The following aspects are also very much important in the successful implementation of inclusive education in public schools.

Legal action and legislation:
The government is expected to provide legal act and legislations to foster inclusion and equity for education and schooling of all the group of children in the public education system. This implies that the educational policies must address the rights of every child based on the supportive approach of legislation. For example, the government of India, has shaped its National Education Policy that is embedded with the essence of inclusion based on the Right to Education to all and the persons with disabilities (PWD) Acts covers all the rights pertinent to people with disabilities. The government also sets up agencies like the Rehabilitation Council of India (RCI) and national institutes for disabilities, which ensures the smooth implementation of education throughout the country.

*****

Inclusion:

Celebrating diversity requires thoughtful inclusion. Everyone must be recognized and appreciated for their talents, be provided with opportunities to get involved, and have their perspectives valued and heard.

Courtesy: Chally.com

Section: 7
Strategies to Challenge the Challenges
Strategies for Effective Equity and Inclusion in Education

Section: 7
Strategies to Challenge the Challenges
Strategies for Effective Equity and Inclusion in Education

Units:

7.1. Challenges of National Education Policy

7.2. Background of Inclusive Education in India

7.3. Projected Data on Children with Disabilities

7.4. Major challenges to address

Section: 7
Strategies to Challenge the Challenges
Strategies for Effective Inclusion and Equity in Education

India is a fast-moving economy in the world, and this country has proved its advancement in all the sectors to be a developed nation. The country has offered enormous opportunities for the overall development of children with special educational needs by offering equal opportunities, protecting their rights and by offering full participation in social life like any other child. The Persons with Disabilities Act (PWD Act 1995) and the National Education Policy of India emphasized the importance and rights of children with special needs and their inclusion in the public education system. The New National Education Policy of India (NEP 2020) has also enhanced a lot of rights and amenities for the improvement of children with special needs in public education and inclusion of all categories of children in the mainstream.

7.1. Challenges of National Education Policy

The National Education Policy of India highlights education as the single greatest tool for achieving social justice and equality. Inclusive and equitable education is an essential goal to create an equitable society in which every citizen can dream, thrive, and contribute to national development. NEP visualize that our education system must aim to benefit Indian children, so that, no child loses any opportunity to learn and excel because of circumstances of birth or background. NEP indicates that the Indian education system and successive government policies have made steady progress towards bridging gender and social category gaps in all levels of school education. Socio-Economically Disadvantaged Groups (SEDGs) are broadly categorized based on gender identities (particularly female and transgender individuals), socio-cultural identities (such as Scheduled Castes, Scheduled Tribes, OBCs, and minorities), geographical identities (such as students from villages, small towns, and aspirational districts), disabilities (including learning disabilities), and socio-economic conditions (such as migrant communities, low income households, children in vulnerable situations, victims or children of victims of trafficking, orphans including child beggars in urban areas, and the urban poor). This section discusses the desirable Strategies for Effective inclusion and equity of children with disabilities and special educational needs in the Indian context.

7.2. Background of inclusive education in India

As per the studies of Government of India (Dr. Anupriya Chadda), the concept of inclusive education in India has emerged in early 1960s by accepting children with visual and hearing impairment in mainstream schools. Earlier, the special schools were considered as the only option for educating children with special needs. The first initiative for integrated education of government of India was in the year 1974 through the project 'Integrated Education of Disabled Children (IEDC). In the year 1987, Government of India has initiated another project known as Project Integrated Education for the Disabled (PIED) with the support of United Nations Development Programme (UNDP). Thereafter union and state governments of India have initiated various projects to accept children with special needs in the mainstream and inclusive education became the inevitable part of public education program in India.

Following are the key milestones of inclusive education development that had caused the since the government accepted the new concept of inclusive education.

- 1960's : Emergence of inclusive education in India
- 1974 : Integrated Education of Disabled Children (IEDC)
- 1986 : National Policy on Education
- 1987 : Government of India has initiated Project

- 1992 : Integrated Education for the Disabled (PIED) Rehabilitation Council of India Act
- 1994 : District Primary Education Program initiated IEDC
- 1995 : Persons with Disabilities Act (PWD Act):
- 1999 : National Trust for the Welfare of Persons with Autism, Cerebral Palsy, Mental Retardation and Multiple Disabilities Act (Act 44)
- 1999 : India Australia Training and Capacity Building Project (IATCBP) of NCERT/MHRD for training in integrated education.
- 2000 : Rehabilitation Council of India Act amendment
- 2001 : Sarva Siksha Abhiyan continued IEDC program
- 2004 : Evaluation of the pilot project "Support to Children with Disabilities:
- 2020 : The National Education Policy (NEP 2020)

All the above initiatives that taken by the Government of India have provided legal support and rights to children with special educational needs to become a part of inclusive public education in India. By the adopted acts offered equal opportunities, protected their right and given full participation and enabled all the students to develop their full potentials without any discrimination.

7.3. Projected Data on Children with Disabilities

As per the Government of India Ministry of Statistics and Programme Implementation National Statistical Office Social Statistics Division (2021), Persons with Disabilities (Divyangjan) in India - A Statistical Profile: 2021, the following is the data available with the government.

- Total Population 1,210,854,977
- Disabled population 2,68,14,994
- Percentage of disabled population 2.21
- At all India level, 7.62% of the disabled persons belonged to the age group 0-6 years.

- The State of Uttar Pradesh is home for the highest number of disabled children (0-6 years).
- The highest percentage of disabled children (5-19 years) presently attending educational institution has been reported from Goa & Kerala (73%)
- The percentage of disabled children never attended educational institution is highest in Nagaland (39%) followed by Assam (35%) *(Source: as per census 2011).*

Following are the key findings based on the survey of persons with disabilities in India conducted during NSS (National Sample Survey Organization), 76th round (July – December 2018).
- Among persons with disabilities of age 7 years and above, 52.2 per cent were literates
- Among persons with disabilities of age 3 to 35 years, 10.1 per cent attended preschool intervention programme.
- Percentage of persons with disability of age 3 to 35 years who were ever enrolled in ordinary school was 62.9 per cent.
- Percentage of persons of age 3 to 35 years with disability who were ever enrolled in special school among those who were not enrolled in ordinary school or were enrolled in ordinary school but were not currently attending was 4.1 per cent.

(Source: National Sample Survey Organization-76th round: 2018)

The above data shows that we need to overcome our limitations and find ways to include more and more children in the mainstream of public education so that we can achieve our vision as the country expects. The government is trying its best to implement policies and projects for the inclusion of children with disabilities in the mainstream. However, the efforts of private and non-government organizations also should come forward with more projects to accept and include the children with disabilities in the society. Effective policy of government and coordinated efforts of private sector should go hand in hand to plan and implement the development projects of children and adult with disabilities in the country.

7.4. Major challenges to address

The following paragraphs discusses about 30 major components that need more attention, to address the issues related to inclusive education of children with disabilities and special educational needs. The author is confident that if we can follow the given strategies, full inclusion and equity will be possible in our public school system by 2030. Most relevant factors are detailed in this section to improve the quality of life, education, empowerment, equal opportunities, protection of rights and full participation of people with disabilities in our country. Appropriate projects need to be developed considering the importance and priority, based on the requirement explained in this section to attain full inclusion of such children in our country.

1) **Data collection and update of status of children**

The data on disability is an important tool for the planning and management of projects for the education and rehabilitation of people with disabilities. Availability of relevant data on disability is a challenge of every nation. India was also facing the data on disability in the recent past. However, the Government of India has initiated data collection of disabilities in the national census of India. Status of disability is an essential component of the national census. Ministry of social justice and empowerment (MSJ& E) had also initiated the data collection of disabilities. As per the Ministry of Statistics and Programme Implementation, Government of India (2018), the prevalence of disability (percentage of persons with disability in the population) was 2.2 per cent. It was 2.3 per cent in rural areas and 2.0 per cent in the urban areas. Prevalence of disability was higher among males than females. As per the experience of this author 3 to 5 percentage of children in the public schools are suffering from physical, sensory, behavior or learning disabilities. It is not practical to have the national census of such children in every year, as it need a lot of task and mechanism in government processes. So, the following practical approach can be followed to collect disability data for the effective planning and management of services for children with special needs and their inclusion in public education.

a) Data collection of children with special needs by district or sub district education authority in the beginning of every school year.
b) Enhance the Anganwadi/ Balwadi/ Women's Group/ Local NGOs for early intervention of children with disabilities and to enroll them in the nearby public schools.
c) Women's groups such as the Self-Employed Women's Association (SEWA), Young Women's Christian Association (YWCA), Shikshan Ane Samaj Kalyan Kendra, Kudumbashree movement, etc. are some of the best examples those who can initiate disability intervention projects for the enrolment of children in school at the early stages.
d) High priority should be given to collect data on total population with disabilities, data of students with special needs, separate data on each category of disabilities, condition of male and female community, education level, vocational level, need and requirement etc.
e) State education should have the access and facilities to analyze the data available every year in the beginning of the academic year and the available data can be used effectively for the management of planning and implementation of needful projects for the inclusion of children with special needs for effective public education system.
f) Key findings of all the data available needs to be shared with all the related government departments to avoid duplication of initiatives. National Sample Survey Organization (NSSO) may use this data for analysis and interpretation, as and when needed along with national census.
g) All the relevant data may be used for the procurement of tools, planning of treatment and related support project implementation.

2) **Human Resources development for support services**
Trained and skilled teachers and supporting professionals are the key factors of success of an inclusive education. Once a child is enrolled in a public school the child should be comfortable and feel safe in the school system. The successful Acceptance, appreciation, skill development and learning opportunities etc. are dependent up on the skills and attitude of the specialist manpower in the school. A conducive environment can develop a positive learning environment. So well trained human resources need to be enhanced in the following areas.

a) Trained Teachers and Teacher Assistants/ Teacher Aides
b) Trained specialists in support services
c) Availability of School Psychologist/ Counsellors
d) Allied health professionals for support services
e) Clinical services for immediate intervention as needed
f) Social workers and social scientists' support
g) Supporting parents support group
h) Effective education leadership
i) Experienced consultants and experts in inclusive education
j) Effective managers/ administrators in the department concerned
k) Well educated and experienced professional with disabilities

It is the responsibility of the government and rehabilitation council of India to make sure the standard of practitioners in service of people with special needs and disabilities.

3) **Parent efforts for Early intervention**

Positive parenting and the involvement of parents in early school enrolment of children with disabilities are the essential components in the quality services for children with special needs. In a structured educational system parents, siblings and community are equally important to support the child in early identification and intervention at the early stages of child development. Experience shows that the achievement of children who are enrolled in education and support services are much better than the late comers. There is a misbelief that the child cannot understand the concepts well as the child is having a specific disability. Due to this tendency the parents have an inhibition to not to enroll the disabled child in school as the other non-disabled child. Such misbeliefs affect the development of the child at the early stage. Only through proper community education the parents can be geared to enroll the children in education and support services. So, parents and community should be aware about all such stakeholders and complementing factors in early education of such children in mainstream schools.

Following are the key aspects of parent involvement in inclusive education.

a) Need to develop desirable communication of parents and school to offer effective schooling for the child with a disability.
b) Parents to be guided properly to develop desirable parenting skills to manage the child with disability in a home setting.
c) Proper orientation needs to be given to parents, siblings, and peer group to manage well and prepare the child to develop adequate survival skills as needed.
d) Education, culture and understanding of the families should be taken care of, while offering home services.
e) Prominent community service volunteers or parents' support group may initiate to prepare the family members for needful orientation on disabilities.
f) Partnership of families as a volunteer in school can enhance the inclusive school to be more effective.
g) Parents group may act as a convergence agency along with the educational authority.
h) Effective parent community can act as a team to support underprivileged parents to educate their children with disabilities at the early stages.

i) Parents' community in school operational management can act as a decision-making factor in supporting children with disabilities.

Authorities and school management should accept and cooperate with parents and their support group to get their maximum support for the early education of children with disabilities and effective inclusion of such children so that the country can achieve a real inclusion as expected.

4) Facility improvement for accepting kids with disabilities

A conducive learning environment is an essential factor for accepting children with special needs in a mainstream school. A child with disability should be equally accepted and welcomed with a positive attitude and supporting mentality. Parents of such children are always stressed due to various negative experiences. So, it is the responsibility of the school and community to provide a flexible facility to accommodate the child in school. It is obvious that a school cannot equip all the facilities required for children with disabilities in the initial stage as the need and nature of children are different. For example, a child with physical disability may require an access free building where a child with hearing may require different facilities. So, considering the need and nature of requirement, the school may adapt and accept physical and environmental changes in the premises as and when required.

Physical infrastructure, accepting environment, positive attitude, curriculum adaptation, enhancing the support of peer group and other parents, offering facilities and concessions as stipulated by the authorities, appropriate transportation facilities, offer assistive technology, getting locally available teaching learning materials, safe and supporting school environment and more over a positive attitude from the teachers and other staff are the basic requirement of children with disabilities in their school accessibility services. It is obvious that a school cannot develop all the facilities well in advance to support the child with disability. However, with the support of education authority, parents' community, supporting staff or through some volunteer group all the facilities can be developed within a short period of time.

5) Positive Culture in favor of inclusion of disabilities

Attitude matters over everything. A cultural change with a positive attitude towards the children with special needs is to be developed in all the private and government educational institutions, schools, universities and working environment. Appropriate authorities and related organizations, government departments and non-government agencies should plan activities to develop a positive culture to accept the people with disabilities in their society. A culture of acceptance of disabilities in the society should be injected in the school going children so that a real inclusion will be possible in the society. The school should be a place where all the children are equally accepted and recognized without any discrimination. Effective inclusion should start from a culture of positive attitude and acceptance. Experience shows that the efforts of few staff and parents with positive attitude made huge changes in many public schools and proved that effective inclusion is possible in our public schools with community support.

6) Grievance Addressing Mechanism

As per the Rights of Persons with Disabilities Act, 2016 (Section 23), every Government establishment shall appoint a Grievance Redress Officer to address issues related to people with disabilities in India. Such an officer has the authority to investigate and take up the matter with the establishment for corrective action. The Grievance Redress Officer is expected to maintain a register of complaints in the manner as may be prescribed by the Government, and every complaint shall be inquired within two weeks of its registration. If the aggrieved person is not satisfied with the action taken on his or her complaint, he or she may approach the District-Level Committee on disability. However, it is evident that the disability issues are not considered as a priority subject in most of the institutions. Thousands of cases in such subjects are still not addressed. A monitoring mechanism should be developed by the central government to speed up the issues. Coordination of school authorities, district and state level officers should be enhanced to develop needful measures to develop a grievance mechanism in all the levels in district, regional, state, and national level. The national authorities should develop standard operating policies and procedures to ensure the grievance addressing mechanism in the country.

7) Decision-Making and Planning

It is important for the government to determine the decision-making authority in each educational institution so that children with disabilities and their grievances can be redressed without any hazards. A single point of contact should be made available to support such children and parent whenever they face crisis. Timely intervention in case of rejection, enhancing the child for proper education, empowerment, social acceptance, and participation in daily life like other children should be supervised by such responsible authority so that an effective inclusion can be expected. Along with education, employment, and rehabilitation are the national subjects, a competent authority should be available to make sure to empower them as a single point of contact. Such authority should be established in all the schools, departments, and organizations to address the disability related issues as a human right issue. The National Education Policy and the Rights of Persons with Disabilities Act, 2016 highlights the importance of competent authorities for the redress of issues related to disabilities.

8) Communication Channel

Support Services and timely communication are equally important in the disability service sector. Hence a framework needs to be established in terms of the disability service. Appropriate government and non-government agencies should mutually develop a time frame for their spectrum of services. A nodal officer for disabilities may be assigned in every administrative region. School region and school authorities should have frequent access to such monitoring and consulting officers or agencies so that everyday operational issues related to disabilities can be addressed on time. Experience shows that there are many duplications in support services as there is lack of coordination in planning and management of services. It is noticed that different agencies are implementing similar projects in education and rehabilitation at the same time. Such duplication causes drain of brain and funds, and the real beneficiaries do not get the services as required. So, it is always needing a proper communication channel at the national, state, regional or district level for all the projects related to the education and empowerment of children with disabilities.

9) Scholarship and financial assistance
To provide equal opportunities and equity for the children with disabilities in public education, it is necessary to provide appropriate scholarships and financial support mechanisms. The child with a disability is mostly denied their opportunities as the institutions are not equipped with basic facilities. Most of the families are unable to pay for basic rehabilitation facilities as it is very expensive. Early detection facilities, treatment and technology-based tools and equipment costs high in the country, as we do not have sufficient insurance facilities. Though, the government is providing free treatment in many states the quality of services is yet to be improved. The service of non-government agencies in the country needs to be appreciated as they are providing enormous support in disability rehabilitation. Unfortunately, the number of beneficiaries is very less out of our huge population. So, a mechanism to provide scholarship and financial support is to be developed jointly by the government, non-government, and the corporate agencies in every region in the country so that maximum coverage can be done to bring all the children with disabilities in the country under the spectrum of educational services. Following are the key areas that a child with disabilities needs financial assistance for:

- Early detection of impairment and disabilities
- Early preparation services
- Medical treatment and allied health support services

- Basic tools and equipment (hearing aids, optometric, prosthetic, orthotics, tools)
- Course fees
- Technical appliances
- Therapy services
- School expenses
- Living expenses in case of financially deprived families
- Transportation
- Merit scholarships for high achieving students
- Higher education support

Experience shows that malpractices are evident in the disability service sector. So, the appropriate authorities must develop eligibility conditions for Scholarship and it should be strictly followed. Participation of government and private sector should be enhanced in scholarship support and needful standard of practices also needs to be developed for adequate scholarship system in the country.

10) Not-for-Profit Organizations

Non-government and Not for Profit Organizations are the channelizing agents for proper care, education, and inclusion of children with disabilities. The institutional cares offered by the government agencies is gradually declining these days as the government institutions have limitation to address the educational needs of all the children with special educational needs. So non-government organizations play a crucial role in the service of children with disabilities for effective inclusion in our public education system. There are number of non-governmental organizations with great track record for the service of disabled people in our country. If they can collaborate with the government, the welfare services would become considerably better than at present. The government cannot go to grassroots levels to understand and address the local issues and requirement of children in every region. So, only through local organization can they identify the local requirement and work for the effective inclusion of children considering the need and nature of the society. Involving parents and the community is an important principle of quality, inclusive education, both in and out of the school environment. A local organization can develop a positive connection between parents and schools to develop positive attitudes and achievements in inclusive education. Such involvements of different stakeholders make a huge difference and adds value to parents, classmates, educators, and schools. Following are the expected roles and benefits of Not-For-Profit Organizations for creating effective inclusion of children with special needs in our public education system:

- Early detection survey/ case studies / need assessment
- Keeping track of the identified children
- School advocacy
- Arranging local resources
- Parents support and awareness
- Empowerment
- Community based rehabilitation
- Vocational rehabilitation and training
- Assistive technologies
- Self-employment and microfinance
- Volunteer service
- Well-being of people with disabilities
- Break the language and cultural barriers
- Improve the cooperation between schools, teachers & community
- Pre-school education
- Address social issues
- Pre-vocational training
- Effective use of social media support
- Identifying child need and ensuring their placement
- Fundraising for effective support services

Structured monitoring system, convergence and effective coordination between government and private agencies are required for the effective support services in favour of inclusion and equity of children with special educational needs.

11) Code of Conduct

A code of conduct refers to the standards of professional conduct that promotes effective equity and inclusion in our school system. It provides a framework for all the stakeholders to support day to day ethical decision making in educational setting. A code of conduct for the parents, teachers, support professionals and public who are dealing with disabilities at the national level needs to be framed to develop a positive attitude and full inclusion. This will improve the acceptance of such people to get equal opportunities, protection of rights and full participation in the community life. UNESCO highlights the following elements as the code of conduct for effective inclusion.

- Identification and removal of barriers to learning
- Have all students achieve results in attendance
- Participation in all school activities
- Quality learning

An effective inclusive should accept the diversity and should create an effective learning environment. The following are the suggested code of conducts to improve an effective school environment where the child will be well accepted and respected.

- Treat all the children impartially without discrimination with regards to ethnicity, disability, sexual orientation, language, economic status, geographic factors, religious, caste, spiritual beliefs, and political beliefs.
- Avoid stereotype attitude and prejudice
- Interact with them in an open minded, compassionate, and positive manner
- Do not use any negative tones hinting their disability in classrooms
- Accept the diversity in achievement level of different children
- Always be an advocate for a child with disorder
- Encourage peer tutoring and cooperative learning atmosphere
- Share the tool and equipment as much as possible

- o Engage other staff and parents to resolve complaints or conflicts
- o Avoid aggressive behavior towards special children including mental, physical, and verbal abuse.
- o Keep personal information confidential and follow a standard policy in confidentiality of records
- o Report unethical or illegal behavior or practices to the authority

To keep the standard of professional conduct and practices, needful policy, procedure, and standard of practices should be prepared covering all the aspects related to children with disabilities. Proper monitoring is also suggested by an internal or external quality management agency to ensure the quality practices for effective inclusive education.

12) Organizational Size & Structure

We have different type of organizations such as organizations for disabilities and organizations run by people with disabilities. Disabled Peoples' International (DPI) considers the role of organizations of disabled people to be the most fundamental issue for the disabled person's movement. As a vehicle of self-development, these organizations provide the opportunity to enhance the identification of children with special needs, their education, empowerment, vocational training, advocacy etc. it is evident that all the organizations cannot focus on all the activities required for support services. So, the nature of services, organizational size and structure need to be identified to enhance the organization, to avail government assistance and to ensure quality management in dedicated services. High-level institutions may extend support to undertake huge and long-term projects in the disability sector and small organizations maybe assigned with small projects considering the local needs. The cooperation of large and small organizations is very much required to identify the local needs. The following are the different structures of reputed organizations that offer services for the development of education and rehabilitation of people with disabilities:

- International organizations
- National organizations
- Regional institutions
- Government agencies and departments serving disabilities
- Public and private institution supporting education of special needs
- Schools and universities offering education

The following are the key areas to focus on by organizations, for effective inclusion in the coming decades:

- Develop scope of services
- Societal attitude modification
- Awareness and public education on disability issues
- Medical, allied health and rehabilitation support services
- Community based rehabilitation
- Establish services centers for specific disabilities
- Charity, empowerment, and advocacy services
- Grass root services
- Network of services connecting beneficiaries
- Evaluating, monitoring, accreditation & quality management of services
- Funding agencies

Irrespective of the size and structure of organizations, all the agencies should cooperate with each other in identifying the needs of children with disabilities for their inclusion in educational environment.

13) Self-help organizations for inclusion

Self-help organizations are supporting children with disabilities in boosting the efforts for public education at a large scale in India and other developing countries. Most of such organizations are focusing on the education, employment, and rehabilitation of single category disability services. According to the United Nations estimations, not more than 2-3 per cent of the disabled people who need rehabilitation are receiving required services. Lack of participation of parents, self-representation of people with disabilities and the lack of self-help organizations are the reason for such situation. This condition highlights the importance of such organization in enhancing the participation of children with disabilities in public education. The World Programme of Action stressed the role of such supporting establishments and organizations of disabled persons to facilitate the participation of disabled persons and their organizations in decision making in disability related services.

Following are the expected services from self-help organizations in favour of inclusive education:
- Identification of children with disabilities
- Develop self-determination in children with disabilities
- Empowerment of disabled children and their parents
- Resource mobilization and financial assistance
- Guidance, counselling, and facility improvement
- Link with schools, hospitals and other professional organizations and closely working with government agencies and other NGO's
- Volunteering in support services
- Arranging peer, parents, and community support to empower children with disabilities
- Creating a supporting and accepting environment in schools and community

Considering the specialization that each organization is focused on, emphasis can be given to support in specific area of disabilities. Thus, such self-help organization can be a local pilot agency for creating an effective inclusive society.

14) Social Inclusion and Economic Participation
Full inclusion and participation should be the major aim of every organization serving in the disability sector. With the available facilities and infrastructure, it is unable create special institutions for all the children with disabilities. So, all such children should be accepted in public schools. Severe disabilities can be enrolled

in the specialized institutions. Economic independence is one of the solutions for social acceptance. People with disabilities and their families need to be enhanced with economic independence and they should be supported well to boost the inclusion of the child. Hence economic viable projects need to be planned for the improvement of the economic condition of people with disabilities, especially those who belong to the economically weaker sections.

There is a need to increase the basic social welfare services, auxiliary or allied health services to accept the child once it is identified as having a disability. An effective social welfare system will deliver better results for the disadvantaged groups. Local government and non-government agencies need to undertake adequate projects to improve the social inclusion and economic support to such socially disadvantaged groups.

15) Flexible & Innovative

Use of innovative technology in classroom is a great capital for the improvement of children with disabilities in inclusive schools. Flexible and innovative technology can be a super mechanism for the improvement and acceptance of all the children in public education. Creating innovation in learning in the physical and virtual mode is the need of hour during and the covid-19 pandemic. Virtual education and technology have become a catalyst for education these days. Flexible and innovative technology is an essential factor for special children too. So In order to incorporate all children in the mainstream alongwith their regular peer group, we must concentrate on sophisticated learning methodology and technology. Education, medical, rehabilitation and educational technologies advances rehabilitation and inclusion in the best possible way. Government and non-government agencies need to develop new technologies and adapt indigenous technology for the inclusion. In this era of most scientific advancement, artificial intelligence is changing the way that we educate our children. In the field of special education, many children with disabilities are currently being underserved due to the lack of technology. Such technology in education can boost the condition of disabilities and non-disabilities equally in schools while they share the learning technologies.

Following are some of the benefits of innovative technology that can enhance inclusive classrooms more effective:

- Maximum engagement, collaboration, and participation in activities
- Enhance academic improvement
- Enhance learning interests
- Minimize the time and efforts to achieve the goals
- Make the child independent in completing tasks
- Improving the productivity, creativity, and effectiveness
- Addressing equal participation and diversity in learning
- Making easy curriculum transaction
- Enhancing life skills
- Helping all to accommodate multiple learning styles
- Support equally to prepare everyone in the classroom for their future.

By adapting suitable and innovative technology a public school can easily accept children with disabilities in the mainstream classrooms and improve their quality of learning and independent life.

16) Local Connections and local responsiveness

Local agencies and facilities are the major instruments for effective inclusive schooling. A meaningful inclusive education system should accept all the children irrespective of special needs and disabilities in the local school. Enhancing all the schools to use the local resources in favor of education and rehabilitation of disabilities is a challenging task. Community based rehabilitation and community-based education are the key facets in support services. So, the proper utilization of local resources, participation of local community, community organizations, local resource persons, community leaders etc. play a crucial role in education of children with disabilities. Each stake holder shares equal responsibility of addressing the educational needs of a child with disability. With the participation of local resources, the child can be easily enrolled in their local schools.

The following are the key aspects in using local connections and local responsiveness:
- The facilities and assets available in the local community
- Community's ability to address the requirement
- Cooperation and support of community
- Participation of the community members in favour of inclusion of all their society
- Cultural and political responsibility
- Family and society relation
- Local leaders and community volunteering
- Sharing of resources and financial support
- Accepting the community diversity
- Crating a barrier free and bullying free society

A responsible community can easily identify the need of children with disabilities and accept all with their diversity.

17) Stakeholders

As explained earlier community is a key stakeholder in accepting children with disabilities in their society. Other key stakeholders such as government, ministries, local administration, school authorities, community leaders, volunteers, professionals etc. are also equally important in support services. All the stakeholders must be included in the planning management of rehabilitation support services and inclusive education support. More coordination of the following is very much required to create a conducive environment for children with special needs.
- Regular class teachers and head of the school
- Specialized professionals
- Physicians and allied health professionals
- Parents, sibling, and family members
- Community leaders and volunteers
- Education authorities and managers
- Local administration authority

- Local organizations
- Children with special needs or their representatives
- Media and cultural clubs
- Local funding agencies

18) Monitor Anti-competitive Practices

Unhealthy practices and competition in the private sector and non-governmental agencies are evident in the disability service sector. Some funding agencies have reported that corruption also identified in the service sectors. So, such unhealthy practices need to be controlled and all such organization to be brought under strict monitoring and ensure the cooperation for enhancing best practices for the welfare of people with disabilities and their inclusion.

19) Investment in Research and Evaluation

Universities are mostly undertaking research projects in various areas related to rehabilitation. Some of the scientific and medical organizations are also associated with research projects. Though we have made scientific advancements in rehabilitative technology, we are sadly dependent on other nations for the majority of these developments. More research and development should be initiated by our national organizations so that indigenous technology can be provided to the needy people. Government and corporate sectors need to come forward to invest more on research and development projects in education and rehabilitation of children with special needs along with proper evaluation and monitoring in the disability and rehabilitation sector under the National Commission and related agencies. Proper evaluation and monitoring are also required for research and development in rehabilitation.

School/university students and local organizations may be motivated to do innovative research or develop flexible and innovative invention to support people with disabilities. The best innovation maybe highlighted at the national level and may recognize such students and may provide scholarship for further research.

20) Ensure safety at school environment

Children with disabilities who are enrolled in the school should be safe and secure in hazard free movements and free from other emotional disturbances. PWD Acts and national education policies offers barrier free architecture of buildings and physical infrastructure. However, the psychological condition of the children should be taken care. Bullying, teasing, discrimination, labelling are the negative psychological factors affecting negatively in favour of inclusion. Hence, the local and school authority should be closely monitoring the following:

- Safety and security of children in school
- Strict monitoring against bullying and discrimination
- Avoid labelling
- Remove architectural barriers
- Establish peer group support group
- Promote parents support group
- Ensure insurance for the children
- Reduce the time limit in case of hyperactivity
- The child may be referred to a specialized institution if once cannot be safe or not educable in a mainstream school

The child and parents should feel safe in school so that an effective inclusive environment can be created in mainstream school.

21) Fit-for-Purpose School Conditions

It is the responsibility for school to make sure that the children with disabilities are getting need based education and training. Only an educable and trainable child should be enrolled in a regular classroom. If the child cannot be educated in mainstream, such child should be referred to some care service or skill development training program. All the children with disabilities should be provided with an individualized education program (IEP) that covers all the academic, skill development, and support services considering the peculiar nature of disabilities. If the basic facilities are not available to address the educational needs of a peculiar group of disability, the child will not be getting proper education. In case of an odd environment the child will not get any learning opportunities and it will spoil his/her progress. So, the school environment should be fit for the child.

22) Create Flexible adaptive learning environment

Flexibility is a key quality of an effective inclusive education. Teacher and curriculum should be flexible so that the child can accept the purpose and methodology of teaching and learning. All the children should be prepared to tolerate the changes in classrooms. They should not expect the same level of progress for all the children as their cognitive and functional level are different. When a child with a specific disability is enrolled in the classroom, some of the skills may not be achieved for them considering the physical, sensory, or learning disorders. So, the school structure should be flexible in managing time frame, curriculum, achievement expectation, learning tools and equipment, group activities etc. more than academic ranking focus should be given to life skill development.

The following aspects should be considered and kept in mind to create an effective learning environment:

- Focus on the learning skills, not on the physical disability
- Prepare the children to achieve the maximum as per their cognitive and functional level
- Develop problem solving skills
- Train them to accept diversity in the learning experience
- Develop self-help skills
- Learn to share and care with each other
- Share the tools and equipment for learning
- Enhance cooperative learning and peer tutoring
- Develop partnerships in activities and understand their uniqueness
- Appreciate the success in learning
- Let each child understand their strength and weakness and motivate them to overcome their limitations

23) Life skills Education / Vocational Training Preparation

World Health Organization (1997) defines Life Skills as abilities for adaptive and positive behaviour, which enable individuals to deal effectively with the demands and challenges of everyday life. Described in this way, skills that can be said to be life skills are innumerable, and the nature and definition of life skills are likely to differ across cultures and settings. However, analysis of the life skills field suggests that there is a core set of skills that are at the heart of skills-based initiatives for the promotion of the health and well-being of children and adolescents. Children with special educational needs and disabilities are also expected to acquire such skills to face the everyday life. Following are the key skills expected from a child with disability like any other child to be independent in the society:

- Daily living skills
- Social interaction
- Decision making
- Problem solving
- Creative thinking
- Critical thinking
- Effective communication
- Interpersonal relationship skills
- Leisure and recreational skills
- Functional academics
- Use of assistive technology
- Self-awareness
- Empathy
- Coping with emotions
- Coping with stress
- Pre-vocational and vocational skills etc.

Life skill skills development for children with disabilities and students with special needs are very important and valuable for them to get in education and social life. Such skill development should be a part and parcel of the mainstream educational program. By learning the above skills children with special needs can gain perceptual experience, appreciative experience, and creative experience. All such experiences are required to develop desirable pre-vocational skills, so that a child with disability can be prepared to be trained in any suitable vocational areas based on the nature of disabilities, interest, and aptitude of the child.

24) Financial Assistance

It is always needed to monitor the economic condition of the family of a child with disabilities. Poor people with disabilities need to be provided with financial assistance to do the early intervention support once a child is identified with a disability. It is obvious that there are many government schemes to support families and children, but the service availability may be delayed due to various formalities and process time. So, support from their own community and local government are very much essential to offer services without delay. Social organizations must respond to support such families during such crisis period by offering needful financial and moral support so that the families can have the courage to face the challenges occurring due to the onset of disability of the child. Community and social organization may support affected families in the following areas:

- Financial assistance for treatment to reduce handicapping condition
- Support for allied health services if any
- Follow up for treatment
- Financial assistance for assistive technology
- Financial assistance to family members who are missing their employment to support the child
- Scholarship and concessions for study materials
- Transportation facilities
- Maintenance of supporting devices
- Vocational training
- Hostel fees or living expenses
- Transportation allowance
- Vocational training
- Pre- job training preparation

- Tax reduction for families of disabilities
- Salary of assistants if any

Through the financial assistants the community can empower the affected families to enhance the child in community life and inclusive schooling.

25) Insurance schemes for child with disabilities and their families

It is evident that disability support services cost very high in all the countries since early detection through treatment and follow up services. So, it is always advised to bring all the children with disabilities and special needs under suitable insurance scheme. It is always difficult to decide the 'eligibility' for complete health care and long-term services and support for such children. Once identifies with a disability among children, parents run pillar to post for services that are very costly. Also, the parents may sacrifice their income as they are busy accompanying the affected children. Treatment, assistive devices, therapy supports etc. are high costing and need to be provided without any delay. All children with disabilities should benefits the services and benefits aimed at facilitating access to nutrition, treatment, education, social care, safety, and security. So, the government, local authorities and educational institutions must take collaborative efforts to provide insurance support to such children. The following are the key areas to be considered under insurance services:

- Medical clinics and hospital services to affected children
- Appropriate transport to enable them to seek medical care
- Aid to provide physical support
- Provide mobility devices
- Communication devices
- Service for autism and hyperactive children for behaviour support and therapy
- Assistive tools and aides for education and daily living
- Support for special health care needs

- Medications requirements
- Therapies and allied health services
- Counselling and behaviour services
- Pre-vocational training
- Maintenance of tools and equipment

26) Safe and secure housing facilities

Safe and secure housing facility is the basic need of every individual. People with disabilities also require a decent life and residence facilities like any other person in the society. As parents are spending a lot of money for the treatment and rehabilitation, they may face crisis to establish a safe living condition. So, the government or local authorities may take needful steps to offer housing facilities for people with disabilities for safe settlement and help them to lead dignified lives. Though there are various schemes for housing services, experience shows that thousands of families are still struggling for basic facilities in our country. So, the government and private agencies should come forward to provide housing facilities so that we can develop an inclusive society where a child with disability also well accepted like their peer group in school. All the children should feel that they have a secure home condition. The following are the key aspects to consider for establishing safe and secure home conditions:

- Financial assistance to low-income families to construct house
- Free housing facility for poor families
- Priority in bank loan
- Interest free house loans
- Grant in aid one-time financial assistance
- Rental assistance and down payment assistance
- Concessions in government-owned housing
- Electrification and plumbing facilities
- Adaptation of infrastructure for barrier free accessibility
- Assistance for bills and upkeep of communal areas for shared houses

- Support for accommodation, meals, personal care, and social needs in case of severe disabilities

Feeling of safe and secure home condition will improve the confidence of the child with disability to be a part of effective social life in society.

27) Social Protection & Building Safer Communities

Children with disabilities should be safe as any other child in the society and school system. When the child stays with their families it enables them to be safer than any other places. Inclusive education in a nearby schools provides social protection. A structured environment can develop adequate strategies to improve safety and security of children with disabilities in society and schools. Following are some of the threats, a child with disability is facing in school social environment.

- Bullying
- Physical abuse
- Mental harassment
- Discrimination
- Labelling
- Social isolation
- Negligence of teachers
- Negative attitude from students and teachers
- Negative reaction of peer group and their parents
- Financial troubles
- Lack of support and communication

It is the responsibility of the school authorities to create social protection and safe community living for a child with disability in a public school system.

28) Technology innovation / Assistive technology

Rehabilitation Technology is at the peak of expansion, and it has changed the lives of people in all the walks of society. Supporting technology for the education and rehabilitation of children with disabilities had also witnessed phenomenal changes in the past decades as it an inevitable part of the life of people with special educational needs.

Technology in rehabilitation can be divided in to two separate areas:

- Technology for reducing impairment and handicapping condition (Medical)
- Technology that improves the lives of people (Education and Rehabilitation)

The major role of assistive technology lays within any treatment and in reducing the effect of handicapping condition of a child with disability. Such assistive technology covers devices, equipment, instruments, and software, especially produced for persons with disability for early detection of disabilities, treatment, supportive aids for effectiveness of treatment, protecting tools and devices, tools for body functions, materials to prevent impairments, devices need to be used for long time for personal safely and to reduce the conditions occurring due to physical or sensory disabilities.

Education and Rehabilitation technology helps people with disabilities to make things easier in classrooms and daily life. There are thousands of simple devices that help children with special needs to learn effectively and attain knowledge like their regular peers. Devices for teaching and learning in classrooms, equipment developed for specific disabilities, equipment for mobility, communications, home automation, and personal assistive devices etc. are helping them to improve their everyday life. Effective assistive technology helps children with disabilities for easy access to the general curriculum and improving achievement in education. In another words, the first one mentioned above is for life and second one is for survival. In both areas the aim is to improve the potential of people with special needs to achieve their goals through using effective assistive technology.

Effective assistive technology services are required for the following areas to create an effective inclusive education environment.

- Early identification of impairment and disabilities
- Intervention services
- Effective medical support
- Assistive devices for compensation of medical condition
- Support aids for survival, movement, and sensory support
- Devices for early preparation and daily life skills
- Devices for special needs education
- Special equipment for education
- Communication equipment
- Advanced technology for effective life
- Entertainment technology
- Hardware and software for learning

Assistive technologies enhance the children with special needs to improve in curriculum, co-curriculum, survival skills and transition of required services. It is important that our school system should be able to introduce the available technology for the benefit of needy children. Special education teachers and related support service specialist should have frequent contact in designing the requirement of children with special needs. The professionals should acquire the knowledge and experience in using effective technology in an inclusive school environment so that proper services can be offered to children as and whenever required. Selection of assistive technology should be based on the level of disabilities, intelligence level, health condition, skills, attitude, aptitude, learning interest and geographical conditions.

29) Information, awareness, and single point of contact

It is always a challenge for children with disabilities and their parents to get the right information and awareness about the requirement they want whenever required. Disability is an unexpected occurrence in every family. Experience shows that most of the teachers in our public school system are not familiar or aware about the issues faced by such students and parents. So, an inclusive education system must develop an information and awareness system to enhance the client and parents to get effective information about support services. Due to the lack of right information the condition of handicap may worsen, or the education opportunities may be troubled. A single point of contact should be established in every school for parents, clients, and their teachers so that all such stakeholders should be accessed to required services on time. The information services may focus the following areas:

- Early intervention services
- Selection of suitable medical services
- Identify financial and social support for treatment
- Family and client counselling
- Select suitable preparation for early preparation
- Guide the beneficiaries for selecting suitable educational models
- Introduce education and rehabilitation strategies
- Link with government and private agencies
- Arrange volunteer services and allied health services
- Guide for scholarships and concessions
- Introduce authorities for addressing grievances and get needful support
- Guide the teachers for curriculum adaptation and modification
- Coordinate with social agencies
- Link with authorities in education, disability commissions from lower to higher level
- Act as a single point of contact to address any issues related to peculiar disability conditions

Information is the basic right of every person in India. By offering right and timely information on the above areas the child with special needs can be enhanced in a conducive inclusive education system.

30) Quality Management

To reinforce the value of quality services for children with disabilities, every institution must have an effective quality management system. It will reflect the commitment of the school system and its stakeholders while offering the relevant and quality services to improve the rehabilitation and education condition of affected children. A quality management should with the participation of parents and professionals to ensure the best practices in services. The following components needs to be considered in the quality management in inclusive education:

- Various special education support services
- Allied health services
- Required methodology and curriculum transaction
- Outreach services
- Safety and security of the child in school system
- Joint venture programs
- Virtual support/ consultancy
- Capacity building
- Trained professionals' services
- Effective use of assistive technology
- Disability data management
- Consultation/counselling
- Enhancing integration activities
- IEP preparation and monitoring
- Increasing the interactions between families and schools and improving parental skills
- Monitoring to meet the requirements of vision of institution
- Effectiveness of management system.
- Effective operation budget
- Buildings accessibilities and related facilities.
- Encouraging diversity among students regardless of gender, ethnicity, religion, (dis)ability and socioeconomic status.
- Development of proper standard of practices

- o Policy and legislation
- o Monitoring of standard operation procedures
- o Initiate accreditations with external agencies

Quality planning, quality control, quality assurance, and quality improvement are the basic principles of effective quality management in an inclusive educational and rehabilitation services. Through effective quality management all the strategies for effective inclusion and equity in education can be achieved in a short period of time.

By using the provisions adopted by national educational policy 2020, all our institutions should be able to develop a consolidated institutional framework that supports coherent policy implementation, integrated social security administration, and effective regulation and oversight of the system in favor of inclusion of children with disabilities by 2030. Our children with special needs could become more accepted in the society, and they should not be discriminated any more. Let us hand together for an effective inclusion and equity!

"Strategy is about shaping the future."
-Max McKeown, The Strategy Book

*****

Section: 8
Quality Management of Equity and Inclusion

Section: 8
Quality Management of Equity and Inclusion

Units:

8.1. Method of Quality Management

8.2. Importance of Quality Management

8.3. Elements of Quality Management in Education

8.4. Quality Management in Inclusive Education

8.5. Strategies for Educational Development

8.6. Methodologies for Quality Management in Inclusive Education

8.7. The Key Factors Influencing the Success of Quality Management

8.8. Accreditation Program

8.9. Scope & Opportunities for Accreditation

8.10. Mechanisms for Accreditation

8.11. Procedures of Accreditation

8.12. Staff Preparation for Quality Management

8.13. Required Documentation for Accreditation

Section: 8
Quality Management of Equity and Inclusion

Quality management is considered as one of the key components of education and rehabilitation of children in any education system. It is obvious that every child should have the access to get quality services from the respective organization. Experience shows that the quality management of inclusive education in our country is yet to be improved in service systems of inclusive education of children with special needs. Quality management and quality control (QM/QC) is a process to ensure the satisfactory services best available in the organization. QM gives a direction to move forward with certain standards well accepted in the service sector. Customer satisfaction is the end result of quality management system. The service organanazations are expected to follow a certain sequence of standard and process in the operational management to avail the best possible customer satisfaction. A competent authority has to ensure that the service organization is following a set of standards and get a confirmation from a quality accreditation agency to follow such standards. It will enhance the entire culture and excellence in services.

The Rights of Persons with Disabilities Act, 2016 has highlighted the importance of quality services in service of children, however it is uncertain about the ongoing services in the country. National Education Policy (NEP 2020) has also emphasized some practical provisions and amenities for improvement of services for such categories of children in the public education and their inclusion in the mainstream as well. With this provisions, education and rehabilitation services can be more advanced in quality management. Education is the crucial tool for achieving social justice and equality for any group of disadvantaged children. The aim of government is 'no child would be left behind' or miss any opportunity to learn and excel in life because of circumstances of birth or background. Though the Indian education system and several government policies have made steady progress towards bridging the gap, at all levels of school education, the disadvantaged groups are yet to receive quality services in the country. It is the need of the hour to improve the quality of education and rehabilitation support services of all such groups of children to enhance their education and social life in this modern society.

8.1. Method of Quality Management

Quality Management (QM) is an essential aspect of the success of any education programs or services that are designed for the benefit of children in their equity and inclusive education. QM has become an essential factor in the Indian education, especially after the implementation of the NEP 2020. Following are some of the essential processes that needs to be developed for any organization for quality development.

- o *Develop standard process*
- o *Adequate plan of services*
- o *Data of beneficiaries*
- o *Code of conduct*
- o *Policy and procedures*
- o *Standard of practices and guidelines*
- o *Measurement and Analysis of data*
- o *Corrective measures*
- o *Safety and security*
- o *Procurement system*
- o *Material management*
- o *Management System etc.*

To develop India as a human capital of the world, the present system is inadequate in providing the required quality and standard of education. This section illustrates the importance, key elements, needful strategies, methodologies, guidelines and other relevant factors related to the management of equity and inclusive education of all children, who need special support in the Indian education sector.

8.2. Importance of Quality Management

Quality Assurance and Quality Control (QA/QC) are the major aspects of the Quality Management (QM) system. Child development and educational programs need high quality services in all aspects of educational and support service spectrum. The National Education Policy of India (NEP 2020) has emphasized the importance of quality management in education, as in the former decades the education system in India was compromised in quality resulting in the sub-standard quality of inclusive education, which is in all ways inferior in comparison to international standards. The concerned authorities have realized this issue with the system and thus the NEP has highlighted the importance of quality educational leaders, requirement of operative strategies, effectiveness of teacher education programs and the inculcation of essential aspects into every educational program so as to bring quality approach in education development. The most important aspect of the widely accepted global education system is its quality. It comprises the values of, effective curriculum, trained manpower, facilities, infrastructure, quality in governance and management, opportunities for academic improvement, use of effective technology, effective assessment and evaluation, and all related educational facilities in the public education system.

To ensure agreeable quality in higher education, the Govt. of India has initiated formation of the National Assessment and Accreditation Council (NAAC) in the year 1994 and it has marked a national benchmark in the quality management of higher education system in India. However, the weakness in quality management has continued in our inclusive education system, hence the NEP highlighted the establishment of quality management agencies and strategies for the improvement of qualitative school education in India. The NEP has proposed to form an independent State School Standard Authority (SSSA) in every state of India which will be responsible for regulating public and private schools to ensure the quality management in education. NEP has also proposed for developing a School Quality Assessment and Accreditation Framework in association with the National and State councils of education. Such frameworks are expected to improve the quality system in academia, infrastructure, finance and quality teaching and other challenging areas in education development. However, even after many such recommendations, the quality management system for the improvement of children, who face challenges are, yet to develop needed quality management program for their education development, rehabilitation and required support services. The following sections discusses about quality management in inclusion and equity of various groups of children those who are facing challenges in education and social life.

8.3. Elements of Quality Management in Education

Quality management in general education system is expected to begin from the grassroots level considering various aspects of National and

State education system. As education is in the concurrent list in India, both the State and Union authorities play an equal role in ensuring the quality management of various elements in the private and public education sector. Following are the key elements that are needed to improve the general and inclusive education system as a whole:

1. Corporate Governance
2. Organizational Structure
3. Curriculum Management
4. Pre-Vocational Education
5. Cultural Aspects
6. Role and Responsibilities of Professionals
7. Accountability of Staff
8. Transparency
9. Infrastructure and Facilities
10. Control System
11. Monitoring and Evaluation System
12. Performance Evaluation of Students and Staff
13. Creativity & Innovation
14. Non-Curricular Activities
15. Code of Conduct
16. Compliance with National Policy of Education
17. Adaptability
18. Standardization
19. Collaboration with External Agencies
20. Commitment Towards Community
21. Participation of Stakeholders

8.4. Quality Management in Inclusive Education

As indicated above, there are various other services required for children facing challenging special needs. The following are the key services area that need to be considered for quality management in addition to the requirements in the general education system:

1) Multi-disciplinary Medical Assessment
2) Social Workers Assessment Service
3) Pediatric Screening
4) Specialized Assessments in Support Services Disciplines
5) Physiotherapy
6) Occupational Therapy
7) Speech and Language Therapy

8) Audiology Assessment
9) Optometry Assessment
10) Intelligence and Social Quotient Assessments
11) Psychology & Behavioral Assessment
12) Special Education Services
13) Therapeutic Nutrition Service
14) Health Education and Training Service
15) Family Counseling Service
16) Outreach Services
17) Integration Activities.
18) Volunteer Services
19) Post-Cochlear Implant Rehabilitation
20) Rehabilitation Research
21) Training For Staff and Parents
22) Internship of Trainees from Universities.
23) Quality Assurance
24) Virtual Screening for the Remote Cases
25) Virtual Sessions for Client in Support Services
26) Adapted Sports and Games
27) Assistive Technology Etc.

All such services for the clients available in an educational or support service project should be based on best practices and the client's needs. The services also should focus on the vision, mission and the best practices of the institution as per the national policy of education and the policies highlighted in the People with Disabilities Act.

8.5. Strategies for Educational Development

Meaningful and effective business strategy is the basic requirement of any education or business establishment. Equity and inclusion educational support service is a unique area of specialization where a lot of strategies, resources and techniques are needed for effective service delivery. As there are various categories of special children who need a variety of education, training, treatment, therapy, rehabilitation, and related support services at different levels, an operational system is essential for long-term planning and implementation of quality services for all groups of children in the society. To help each child develop to their full potential and actively participate in family and community life, the organization should have a clear vision and mission. The purpose of the strategy should be to provide the best possible high-quality services in inclusion and equity for all categories of children with special needs and their families. The following are the key requirements in the strategic planning for equity and inclusion in the education of children with special needs.

- Vision, mission, objectives of the organization
- Organization and leadership structure
- Program goals and objectives
- Operational plan
- Role and responsibilities of key professionals
- Standard operating procedures
- Financial planning
- Ideal location and accessibility facilities
- Capacity and target population
- Policy and legal aspects
- Admission criteria
- Nature of beneficiaries
- Role of working group
- Time management
- In-service programs
- HR/ Capacity building strategies
- Communication plan & data management
- Key performance evaluation
- Internal and external networks
- Procurement and management of equipment etc.

In addition to the general program management strategies many more supplementary components are also required, considering the needs and nature of children with special needs. They are as follows:

- Goals of the therapy program
- Diagnosis and prognosis
- Therapy techniques and home exercise program
- Coping strategies
- Use of community resources
- Discharge planning and transition of integration of the child within the community,
- Safety aspects at school and home
- Development and advocacy needs
- Consultation & referral services
- Use of assistive technology

- Assessment and evaluation
- Follow up / outreach services
- Service team management
- Scholarship and related concession for the beneficiaries

Strategies and methodologies may vary based on the nature of children, geographical differences, availability of funds, culture and structure of organization etc. All the strategic goals and objectives of the equity and inclusion program should provide a framework for individualized, family centered care and best practices that focus on development of children with challenging special needs. All the strategies should be age and cultural appropriate with the provision of an interdisciplinary rehabilitation pediatric assessment that determines the rehabilitation potential of the child. Each assessment is based on the child's diagnosis and may include but is not limited to -
- The child's physical, psychological, cognitive, behavioral, communication, social and financial, vocational and educational status.
- The child's developmental skills and potential for improvement.

8.6. Methodologies for Quality Management in Inclusive Education

Experience shows that there is absolute lack of quality management system in rehabilitation support services to ensure the right services for inclusion and equity in the education sector. Though there are suitable quality management methodologies in schools and higher education systems in India, needful methodologies and strategies haven't been developed in the field of special needs education sector in India. National Council for Accreditation (USA) and the Council of Accreditation of Rehabilitation Facilities-CARF (USA/Canada/Europe) had developed different operational strategies for the betterment of support service system for children with special needs. Many developed countries have followed such methodologies and got accreditation in the rehabilitation facilities to ensure international standard in quality management. Indian education system also needs to develop such quality management system for support services. The following paragraphs highlight some key guidelines for developing such a system for the entire support service spectrum. Establishing a quality management department with needful staff and facilities are the basic requirements for quality management services. The schools, teachers, professionals and support service centers may use the given methodologies to develop an appropriate quality management structure for the overall improvement of such children and for their effective equity and inclusion in education.

All the organizations should set up a unit or department to take care of the ongoing monitoring and evaluation with sufficient Quality Management facilities. Such a department is expected to perform the following roles mainly:

1. General Role

Improving the quality of services offered to the beneficiaries and their families, the QM department needs to ensure the strongest and most accepted scientific methodologies followed in the support services. Such efforts can guarantee its technical effectiveness, and can ensure the culture of institution that is compatible with the highest national and international quality standards in the services designed for children.

2. Effective Communication

The Quality Department is expected to enhance effective communication system between the departments and sections of the organization. Joint decision-making is always required in order to generalize the quality to all workers by paying attention to the details of performing tasks internally and externally. So that, the overall efforts will be directed towards excellence and continuous quality improvement in all units and departments.

3. Administrative and Technical Efforts:

The Quality Department is expected-to direct the administrative and technical efforts of the organization to achieve the strategic objectives, vision and mission for which it was established. The role and responsibilities of each administrative professional should be well defined and communicated well on time for effective administration of the quality management system.

4. Decision Support Role:

The quality department is also anticipated to work on the decision support by monitoring the quality of operational services, overseeing the participation of all departments and sections in recommendation, and also by observing the development of corrective measures that may include the modification of operational processes and the internal administrative distribution of tasks. The decision support should be based on the results of data analysis, statistics and key performance indicators. Recommendations for facility improvement should be made for each department separately, while determined efforts contribute towards achieving the objectives of the service organization.

5. Develop Policies, Procedures and Standard of Practices

Develop new policies or modify practicing policies, procedures, mechanisms and models by working with the concerned departments, and their efficiency with the scope of service, strategic objectives, as well as global benchmarks and standards. The National / State policies for education and the guidelines of various councils in rehabilitation, medical and education etc. needs to be considered in terms of preparation of policies for each department.

6. Maintaining a Database

Maintaining the needful data, policies, procedures, mechanisms and forms is yet another specific role of the QM department. The Quality Department prepares or approves the policies, procedures, mechanisms and models in the organization in line with its strategic mission, vision and objectives and in line with the international standards organizations.

7. Provide Consultations

The Quality Department should support the departments and sections in formulating and implementing operational plans and amending them in line with the general strategic plan and objectives of the project upon request. Overall evaluation of the center, academic and administrative management, financial aspects, follow-up on general quality management etc. are the other areas that need consultation for improvement. Service of external experts can also be availed for all such consultation services.

8. Client Satisfaction

Client satisfaction survey should be maintained in the quality management by direct contact with a sample of beneficiaries to determine the extent of satisfaction level, general observations and suggestions and take them as possible. This should be done by keeping frequent contact with the clients and by depending on virtual facilities. Sufficient follow up should be done to rectify the issues raised by the clients. Technical monitoring system should be established for the effective follow up of the client satisfaction system.

9. Monitoring of Documentation:

Monitoring of documentation should be done at least in every two months for a sample of specialists by following a standard criterion. All the departments should have sufficient documents and the QM department is expected to ensure that the entire staff are familiar with the documents and the processes concerned with it, in the departments and units. The quality of documents should be at par with the National / International standard and the best practices to ensure that the documentation standards are adhered to by the organization.

10. Administrative Follow-up of Sessions:

This is to be done at least in every quarter to ensure that practices comply with policies related to attendance and recall of beneficiaries, and the commitment of specialists from the commencement to the conclusion of the session.

12. Technical Follow-up of Sessions:

The QM Department should ensure the quality of support services by conducting live visits of the sessions, by expert specialist to make sure the practitioners are offering the quality services as per the plan of the organization. This should be done at least once in every quarter for all specializations through internal or external technical experts to ensure that the actual practices within the session match the approved policies and procedures for setting treatment goals, documenting progress towards them during the service program, educating parents and also align with the exit plan.

13. Follow-Up of the Extended Services Program:

This is expected to be done at least once in every semester by making field visits with the team and conducting follow-ups with the performance according to the expected standards. Surveying and evaluating cases, providing the required therapeutic interventions, providing consultations to teachers, parents and specialists, delivering home programs, guidance to resource centers, if any, and giving recommendations to manage the school-based services with regards to the surrounding environment and making adjustments inside and outside the classroom to help the students achieve academic successes etc., are also considered as the key roles of the quality management department. A variety of broad roles can be undertaken by the QM departments as and when required. Business analysis, studying the organizational needs, outreach programs, effective discussion with stakeholders, develop requests and solutions that give value, strategic planning, reports and statistics preparation, monitoring and analyzing the overall improvement of the project etc., are some of the other expected roles for quality management department. Though, there are many such roles for the QM department, the success of the quality is based on the various factors as follows:

8.7. The Key Factors Influencing the Success of Quality Management

- Tested policy and procedures
- Operation budget
- Suitability of buildings/facilities
- Deployment of suitable management & operational teams
- Selection of qualified professionals
- Selection of suitable sub-contractors, if any
- Maintenance of building
- Geographical coverage
- Accessibility to the services
- Safety and security
- Training facilities
- Development of proper standard of practices (SOP)
- Clinical management system
- Procurement of technical materials
- Deployment of suitable Quality Management team etc.

8.8. Accreditation Program

Accreditation from the national or international agencies is one of the best ways to improve the quality of any support service projects. Such accreditation can improve the overall standard of the project at par with the international and national standard. Accreditation agencies can provide guidance and consultation to the project to improve the overall functions of the project. Agencies such as CARF, ISO, NCASES, NAAC, National Medical councils and rehabilitation councils etc., are some of the prominent agencies that can get accreditation and consultation for quality improvement and standardization in equity and inclusive education support services.

8.9. Scope & Opportunities for Accreditation

Accreditation and certification from the competent authorities are equally important for improving the quality and standard of any organization. Some of the benefits of such accreditations are as follows:

- Accreditation helps in acquiring an international approval from the other known institutions.
- It is considered as an internal system to enhance the quality level.
- It helps the organization to manage the functions at par with international standards.
- Helps to improve the skills of professionals.
- Helps to get ahead of other institutions with international recognition.
- Boost and provide opportunities to meet the requirements of the organization.
- Distinguish the project based on the high standards of practices as per the best international practice and standard.
- Identify the professionals to serve the entire nation.
- Pinpoint how to bridge the knowledge and enhance rehabilitation and inclusive education research.
- High scope of training and capacity building of professionals.
- Enhance virtual support services in support services.
- Develop world class support service system.
- To be the best model project to enhance high quality services.
- Quality Management tools and techniques always helps the institutions to improve competence, efficiency and prosperity of the institutions concerned.
- It helps professionals to improve their skills, abilities, knowledge, and expertise from diagnosis to discharge services.
- Quality management improves the overall efficiency of specialty areas, management and financial effectiveness.

Scope and opportunities may vary from one organization to another.

8.10. Mechanisms for Accreditation

The following areas are generally highlighted by international accreditation agencies to ensure quality management in rehabilitation and special education support services. It is recommended that an annual business calendar be made for quality management and decision support to ensure quality of the rehabilitation support services. In addition to the general quality management components, the following prominent areas are also suggested for quality improvement:

- General quality follow-up (facilities and staff)
- Operational strategy of the organization
- Management structure
- Client satisfaction
- Monitoring the quality of communications
- Monitor use of CCTV cameras / calls / front office etc.
- Administrative monitoring of sessions
- Technical follow-up of sessions
- Follow-up record of beneficiaries after exit
- Accidents and complaints follow-up record
- Risk management and history
- Record of rejected cases, if any
- Wound care record
- Quality of equipment
- First Aid kits
- Periodic maintenance of equipment used in providing the service
- Standards of practice compliance checklist

8.11. Procedures of Accreditation

CARF / ISO / NCASES etc. are some of the major accreditation agencies focusing standardization and accreditation in rehabilitation and related support service programs. There are various needs and nature in requirements to get the accreditations and certification from international agencies. The following procedures are anticipated to be completed while an institution prepares for accreditation.

1. First Step (Documentation):

Development of an operational manual for quality management is the first step towards quality management and is it the key requirement for the accreditation process. The vision, mission, objectives etc. of the institution, service policy, procedures and standard of practices etc. should be established through the operational manual. The institute also needs to set the roles and responsibility of each staff within the institution and providing them the awareness training is yet another requirement for the accreditation journey. Teaching Plan, Organization Chart, Layout and Various Plans, Conducting Internal Audit, Review of Management meetings & the implemented Management System, standard documentation of all the operational, management as well as the educational and support services should be readily available, before commencing the accreditation process.

2. Second Step (Identification of Process):

Generally, the school operation processes mainly focus on administration, curriculum management, allocating spaces for the classrooms, time management, laboratories, workshops, libraries, along with allocating the teaching periods, assessing the performance of the students, designing and developing the validation results of the curricula or the syllabus, developing the course catalogues, developing the course materials, hiring of the administrative and the teaching staff, marketing and the recruitment process, providing of security, safety and the civil protection services, selecting and also enrolling the learners. In addition to the above criteria, the support service programs and its process and policies, should be well defined with the essential processes for the smooth operation of support services. For any accreditation process, all of the above policies and process should be well documented in print as well as digital forms. All the staff should be well trained to follow the procedures as prepared by the institution. The quality management department is expected to verify the above to ensure the smooth functioning of the above-mentioned services.

3. Third Step (Certification Process):

Generally, the certification body may have proper application forms with relevant details. The institution can get sufficient guidelines and information regarding accreditation process with application and payment details. The application and payment should be done after a proper internal auditing to ensure the basic achievement of standards as expected for accreditation. Different organizations have different practices for the process of application.

4. Fourth Step (Technical Review / Certification decision):

After the internal audit, a comprehensive report is required to be prepared and submitted to the accreditation agency for technical review. The organization may suggest needful measures for quality improvement for the ongoing programs. The organization is eligible to get the live evaluation and certification only after various stages of online and offline evaluation.

5. Fifth Step (Certification Cost):

The cost of the certification also varies from organization to organization and also the certification body in general practice. The cost of certification shall thus be derived after considering the number of employees (Full time / Part time / Subcontracted), number of sites or the branch of school education that is covered, under the certification and the number of working shifts.

6. Sixth Step (Selection of Certification Body):

There many Certification bodies globally, but it is also advised to select a suitable certification body for accreditation. The main parameters of the selection are the cost of accreditation, specialty of the accreditation body, accessibility condition, recognition and acceptance of the body in India etc. Though, there are many such agencies globally available, ISO is a well- accepted accreditation agency in India. However, CARF and NASEC are more relevant agencies in terms of inclusion and equity of children with special educational needs.

7. Seventh Step (Certification Training):

Training in the area of specialty provided by the accreditation agency is an essential component in quality management. Each agency will have an operational manual and needful guidelines to the organizations considering the structure and standard of services. The organization is expected to follow and fulfill a set of standards stipulated by the accreditation agencies. So, all such guidelines and instructions should be familiar for the entire staff of the organization. Many such agencies are conducting virtual trainings too, which is very convenient to enroll entire the staff for training.

8.12. Staff Preparation for Quality Management

Quality of the practicing professional is one of the high requirements of the quality management. Qualifications, experience, the process of work, standard of practices, the quality of materials, resource management etc. are some of the key facets in determining the quality of operation of any establishment. All the staff members are expected to be familiar with the following aspects for standard improvement and quality management.

- o Ensure that there is sufficient policy, procedure and guidelines related to the work they are assigned with.

- Refer and study well the standard of practice (SOP) prepared for the specialty with the respective policy, procedure and process, that is available in your department.
- Staff should have the individual work plan of all your clients in your department and get familiar with the plan.
- Be familiar with the Vision, Mission & Goals of the organization.
- Be familiar with the service methodologies, strategies, techniques, tools, teaching learning materials, and equipment that are using in the department.
- All the documents (forms, assessment reports, individual plan, progress reports, brochures, if any, etc.) of each discipline need to be updated.
- Manage time efficiently and effectively with each client and ensure that they are able to utilize the time effectively during the scheduled support service session.
- Be familiar with the online contacts and the external specialists and stay updated with the latest trends in the field of specialty.
- Staying abreast with the best evidence-based practices is extremely essential.
- Customer satisfaction should be the prime aim and make sure that the client and parents are availing the best educational support services from the organization.
- Make sure that the child is getting the best services within the stipulated time.
- Strictly follow the communication channels from the concerned authority and be familiar with the messages / circulars communicated with you from the various departments.
- Take care of the cleanliness, safety, security, health protocols and other safety measures of the clients in the working environment.
- Create a friendly environment for the parents and students, and encourage the client to enjoy their visit for services.
- Feedback should be recorded and follow up should be initiated as per the comments received from beneficiaries.

All the staff members should be able to follow the guidelines strictly for the improvement of standard and quality management, at the stated time of the international accreditation. The quality management department is expected to ensure that the staff members are expected to answer most of the following questions, while focusing on the quality improvement of the organization.

1. What is the Mission, Vision and objective of your organization?
2. Do you have a Standard Operation Procedure (SOP) for your department?
3. Do you have meaningful term plan, needful facilities and materials?
4. Do you have the appropriate safety and security system for the beneficiaries? If yes, what are the:
    - *Number of emergency-exits?*
    - *Fire extinguisher locations and applicability of its usage?*
    - *Number of assembly points?*
    - *Emergency contact numbers?*
    - *When calling the emergency number, what information should be given to the emergency officer?*
5. Do you have color code system and what each color of the emergency codes means?
6. How to deal with cases of violence and hyperactive children?
7. Do you know how to report incidents and the escalation process?
8. Do you know how to escalate a client complaint against an employee?
9. Do you know how to escalate an employee complaint against a client family?
10. Do you know how to escalate an employee complaint against another employee or the supervisor?
11. Do you know how to deal with client emergency cases?
12. Do you know health protocols (as in Covid precautions)?
13. Do you know how to prepare policies, procedures, and process for your department / unit?
14. Do you know the client's rights and responsibilities?
15. Do you know the educational rights of children with special needs in India?
16. Are you familiar with the National Education Policy?
17. Do you know the educational provision of backward children under PWD Act?
18. Are the appliances / equipment regularly serviced? Do they work as required?
19. Are the materials used in the sessions valid and not expired?

20. Do you know the mechanism of referring cases to external services?
21. Do you know the admission, transfer, and discharge criteria?
22. Do you have a suitable virtual service guidelines and criteria?
23. What are the precautionary measures to protect against pandemics?
24. What are the skin integrity and wound care procedures?
25. How do you manage the Individual Education Plan (IEP) or term goal for the beneficiaries?

There is a well-accepted way of process in quality management and accreditation. So, the staff members should be extremely dedicated in the organization, on the occasion, when they are getting ready for quality improvement or accreditation process. The entire staff should be flexible, interactive, and consistent with a clear plan in mind, focusing on the progress of the client in the organization. The monitoring team should observe and prepare the progress note for every activity and needful intervention should be there on every aspect concentrating on progress. Always highlight the positive side of progress as far as possible, to ensure quality and rectification of issues from time to time.

8.13. Required Documentation for Accreditation

Documentation is the most important aspect for standardization and accreditation of any education project. All the educational institutions should follow the required policy, procedures, and certain standards for operation of any activity in academic, finance, support services or administration of the institution. All such processes should be well presented and documented in print and digital form in every institution. The head of the institution and the concerned officer in charge of quality management should be equally responsible for the management of quality and standard of the institution. The following are some of the key documents that are essential for the quality management of any organization in education and rehabilitation of children with challenging special needs.

Following are the documents (sample) needed for quality management of effective equity and inclusive education and such documents are the essential components for accreditation and certifications.

Management	Technical
1. Operational Strategy	1. Operational Guidelines
2. Scope of Service	2. Educational Plan for Every Year
3. Organizational Structure	3. Admission Criteria
4. Leadership Structure	4. Brochures / Information
5. Succession Planning	5. Care Plan / IEP / With Smart Goals
6. Funding	6. Standard of Practices
7. Financial Planning & Policy	7. Format and Forms for every Department
8. General Quality Guidelines	8. Checklists For Evaluation
9. Legal Documents	9. Format Of Individual Plans
10. Roles & Authorizations	10. Medical Report Formats
11. Job Descriptions	11. Education Report Formats
12. Staff Master List	12. Assessment Formats
13. External Contracts	13. Referral Forms
14. Signed Agreements	14. Feedback Evaluation Policy
15. Service Level Agreements	15. Case Study
16. Achievement Status	16. Client Screening Form
17. Personal Rights & Responsibilities	17. Advice / Referral
18. The Accessibility Plan & Policy	18. Progress Notes
19. Storekeeping Policy	19. Treatment Goal KPIs
20. Material Management	20. Material Management
21. Employee Management	21. Policy For Assistive Technology
22. Authorizations / Approvals	22. Work Place Competency Policy
23. Operational Calendar	23. Virtual Service Policy & Procedures
24. Code of Ethics	24. Time Management
25. Technology Management	25. Strategies / Techniques / Tools Used
26. Session Database & Analysis	26. Home Service Policy & Reports
27. Key Performance Indicators	27. Evaluation Records / Parents' Feedback
28. Manpower Status Report	28. Corrective measures taken / Follow up services
29. Complaint & Incident reports	29. Outreach Services – Records
30. Maintenance management	30. Updated Records- Forms, Formats & other documents
31. Monthly / Annual Reports	
32. License & Permissions	

The above documents are the required essentials for certification as per the need of various accreditation organizations. The quality management department is expected to enlist and verify the list of documents from time to time as per requirement. Such list of documents itself indicates the quality of any effective organization in education that can provide effective equity and inclusion of deserving children in a progressive nation.

*****

Section: 9

APPENDIX

"Siblings too are important to ignore because no one logs more hours and minutes with special needs children than their brothers and sisters, with the exception of the parents, usually the mother."

Don Meyer

References

1. *A Manual of Policies, Procedures and Guidelines, British Columbia, 2013, Ministry of Education, Victoria British Columbia, Canada*

2. *American Physical Therapy Association (Scope of practice in Physical therapy)*

3. *American Speech-Language-Hearing Association. (2001).* Scope of practice in speech-language pathology. *Rockville, MD: Author.*

4. *Akhil S. Paul (2020), Deaf-Blindness, Sense India International, Ahmedabad, India*

5. *Anon, (2017). [online] Available at: http://www.asha.org/PRPSpecificTopic.aspx?folderid=8589935327&section=Treatment [Accessed 17 Jul. 2017].*

6. *A Report by Pricewaterhouse Coopers LLB (PwC) 2012, An Evaluation of the Special Education Support Service (SESS) Department of Education and Skills, PricewaterhouseCoopers International Limited, UK*

7. *Association for Professionals in Infection Control (APIC) and Epidemiology, Inc. (2009). Chapter 66: Rehabilitation services. In APIC Text of infection control and epidemiology (3rd Ed.)*

8. *CARF 2010, Medical Rehabilitation Standards Manual, CARF, Canada*

9. *Children, L. (2017). Language disorder - children: MedlinePlus Medical Encyclopedia. [online] Medlineplus.gov. Available at: https://medlineplus.gov/ency /article/001545.htm [Accessed 17 Jul. 2017].*

10. *Disability Bill (2012), Government of India, New Delhi*

11. *Documentation Guides – Occupational Therapists, 2010. BlueCross BlueShield, Kansas, 1133 SW Topek, a Boulevard*

12. *Flasher, L.V., & Fogle, P.T. (2004). Counseling skills for speech-language pathologists and audiologists. Canada: Thompson Delmar Learning.*

13. *Great Schools articles, https://www.greatschools.org/gk/articles/making-progress-toward-iep-goals*

14. *Hearing Screening Manual, 2014, Minnesota Department of Health Community and Family Health Division, Child and Adolescent Health Unit*

15. *IATCBP Training Manual, 1999, India Australia Training and Capacity Building Project, University of Melbourne, Australia*

16. *Individual with Disabilities Education Act (IDEA) 1990, the 101st United States Congress, United States of America.*

17. *Jayachandran K. R, 2000, Possibilities Of Inclusive Education In India Based On Successful Integrated Education In Kerala State, Paper presented in International Special Education Conference, University of Manchester, UK*

18. Jayachandran K.R (2002) Employment opportunities for Visually Handicapped in the state of Tamil Nadu, Ramakrishna Mission Vidyalaya College, Coimbatore & CBM International

19. Jayachandran K.R (2003) Job satisfaction of physically handicapped employees in government sector in Southern Sates of India, National Institute of Visually Handicapped, Chennai Regional Centre

20. Jayachandran K.R, (2020), Know Your Child First, Blue Rose Publishers, New Delhi

21. Jayachandran K.R, (2004) Vocational Education of children with special needs, Paper presented in the International Conference On Disability And Rehabilitation, Dubai

22. Jayachandran K.R, (2006), The Challenge, Annual Souvenir, International Indian School & Special Care Centre- Riyadh, Saudi Arabia

23. Jayachandran K.R, PhD & Patrick John 2014, Special Education Feasibility Studies, Riyadh

24. Jayachandran K.R, PhD, 2009, Problems of Integrated Education in Kerala, PhD Thesis, South Gujarat University, India

25. Jayachandran K.R, PhD, 2019, Operational Manual for Special Education Services, Saudi Ministry of Education & Tatweer Education Holding, Saudi Arabia

26. Jayachandran K.R, PhD, 2023, Life Skills Education for Successful Transition to Adulthood of Children with Special Needs, Paper presented in the International Conference on Comprehensive Education, different Arts Center, Thiruvananthapuram India.

27. Keeffe, Jill, WHO Programme for the Prevention of Blindness & University of Melbourne. Dept. of Ophthalmology, (1995), Low vision kit / World Health Organization

28. Leslie E. Packer, Special Education Glossary and Acronyms Guide, 1998 - 2002, published electronically at http://www.tourettesyndrome.net.

29. Lowa Area Education Agencies, Policy Manual, 2014

30. Luterman, D.M. (2008). Counseling persons with communication disorders and their families (5th ed.). Austin, TX: Pro-Ed, Inc.

31. National Council for Special Education Research, 2011, Access to the curriculum for pupils with a variety of special educational needs in mainstream classes

32. National Education Policy, MHRD, Govt. of India 2020

33. Nettina, S. 2006 Lippincott Manual of Nursing Practice 8th Edition

34. NYC Early Intervention Programme Evaluation Requirements Under the Early Intervention Programme, 2003

35. Organizational Effectiveness Audit of the Prince Sultan Centre for Special Education Support Services (PSCSESS), 2015, NOVATEC, Germany & Scheer Management, Tatweer Education Holding

36. Pam Myers, B. (2017). Speech & Language Goals in Preschool -. [online] Child Development Institute. Available at: https://childdevelopmentinfo.com/development/speech-language-goals-in-preschool/#.WH3Un2fNuUk [Accessed 17 Jul. 2017].

37. Person with Disabilities Act. 1995, Ministry of Social Justice and Empowerment, Government of India

38. Play England, Making Space for Play, UK, www.cabe.org.uk.

39. Policies Governing Services for Children with Disabilities July 2014 Table of Contents, Public Schools of North Carolina, State Board of Education, Department of Public Instruction, http://www.ncpublicschools.org/ec/policy

40. Policy Manual 2009, Tennessee Department of Human Services, Division of Rehabilitation Services,

41. Referral to Speech & Language Therapy for school age children, South Warwickshire NHS Foundation Trust, UK

42. Rights of Persons with Disabilities Act, 2016, Government of India

43. Sharma, U. and Deppeler, J., 2005. Inclusive Education in India: challenges and prospects. Disabilities studies quarterly, 25 (1) [online]. Available from: http://dsq-sds.org/article/ view/524/701 [Accessed 8 October 2012]

44. Shipley, K.G., & Roseberry-McKibbin, C. (2005). Interviewing and counseling in Communicative Disorders: Principles and Procedures. Austin, TX: Pro-Ed, Inc.

45. Swaroop, S., 2001. Inclusion and beyond. Paper presented at the North South Dialogue on Inclusive Education, February, Mumbai, India

46. UNESCO, 1994. The Salamanca Statement and Framework for Action on Special Needs Education. Paris

47. The United Nations declaration on the rights of special needs to education, United Nations

48. Turki Alquraini, 2014, Special Education in Saudi Arabia: Challenges, Perspectives, Future Possibilities, Ohio University

49. Volunteer Connections, Volunteer Canada, 2001, Canada

50. Willard and Spackman's Occupational therapy by Barbara A. Boyt Schell

51. World Report on Disability, 2011, World Health Organizations

Abbreviations

For the easy reading, many of the common technical terms are used as short form in this document and following are the abbreviation of the terms.

ADA	:	American Disability Act
ADHD	:	Attention Deficit and Hyperactivity Disorder
ALIMCO	:	Artificial Limb Manufacturing Corporation of India
ASD	:	Autism Spectrum Disorders
AT	:	Assistive Technology
BD	:	Behavioural Disorder
CA	:	Chronological Age
CARF	:	Commission on Accreditation of Rehabilitation Facilities
CBR	:	Community Based Rehabilitation
CCPD	:	Chief Commissioner for Persons with Disability
CP	:	Cerebral Palsy
CCPD	:	Composite Regional Centres for Persons with Disability
CSE	:	Centre for Special Education
CSL	:	Community Supported Living
CWSN	:	Children with Special Needs
DDRCs	:	Districts Rehabilitation Disability Centres
DGET	:	Directorate General of Employment &Training
DIN	:	Disability India Network
DRCs	:	District Rehabilitation Centres
ENT	:	Ear, Nose, Throat
HI	:	Hearing Impairment

HIS	:	Health Information System
ICDS	:	Integrated Child Development Schemes
IE	:	Inclusive Education
IEDC	:	Integrated Education for the Disabled Children
IEP	:	Individualized Education Plan
ILO	:	International Labor Organization
IPH	:	The Institute for the Physically Handicapped
IQ	:	Intelligent Quotient
ISIC	:	Indian Spinal Injury Centre
ISL	:	Indian Sign Language
IYDP	:	International Year of Disabled Persons
KPI	:	Key Performance Indicator
LD	:	Learning Disability
MHRD	:	Ministry of Human Resource Development
MOH	:	Ministry of Health
NAB	:	National Association for the Blind
NCERT	:	National Council for Education and Training
NEP	:	National Education Policy 2020
NGO	:	Non-Governmental Organization
NIDRR	:	National Institute of Disability and Rehabilitation Research
NIHH	:	National Institute for the Hearing Handicapped
NIMH	:	National Institute for the Mentally Handicapped
NIOH	:	National Institute for the Orthopedically Handicapped
NIOS	:	National Institute of open schooling
NIRTAR	:	National Institute of Rehabilitation Training & Research
NIVH	:	National Institute for the Visually Handicapped

NSSO	:	National Sample Survey Organization
OH	:	Orthopedically Handicapped
OPD	:	Out Patient Department
OT	:	Occupational Therapy
PD	:	Physical Disability
PIED	:	Project Integrated Education for the Disabled
PPE	:	Personal protective equipment
PT	:	Physiotherapy
PWD Act	:	Persons with Disability Act 1995
QA/QC	:	Quality Assurance & Quality Control
R&D	:	Research and Development
RCI	:	Rehabilitation Council of India
RRTCs	:	Regional Rehabilitation Training Centres
SEDG	:	Socio-Economically Disadvantaged Groups
SESSC	:	Special Education Support Services Centres
SLP	:	Speech and Language Pathology
SOAP	:	Subjective, Objective, Assessment, and Plan
SOP	:	Standard of Practice
UCBR	:	Urban Community Based Rehabilitation
UNDP	:	United Nations Development Programme
UNICEF	:	United Nations International Children's Fund
UPE	:	Universalizing of Primary Education
VI	:	Visual Impairment
VRCs	:	Vocational Rehabilitation Centres
WHO	:	World Health Organization

*****

Synonyms

Act	:	Disability Act
ADHD	:	ADHD is a mental health disorder that includes a combination of persistent problems, such as difficulty paying attention, hyperactivity and impulsive behavior.
Autism	:	Autism is a condition of uneven skill development primarily affecting the communication and social abilities of a person, marked by repetitive and ritualistic behavior.
Blindness	:	Total absence of sight; or Visual acuity not exceeding 6/60 or 20/200 (Snellen) in the better eye even with correction lenses; or Limitation of the field of vision subtending an angle of 20 degree or worse.
Centre	:	Any Centre where children with special needs get Special education, medical, early intervention and rehabilitation support services
Clinic	:	Rehabilitation Service Clinics
Cerebral Palsy	:	CP is a non-progressive neurological disorder of muscle coordination and control.
Deaf Blindness	:	Deaf-blindness is used to describe a heterogeneous group of children who may suffer from varying degrees of visual and hearing impairment.
Disability	:	Poor performance of daily activities by an individual due to any type of impairment.
Down syndrome	:	It is a genetic disorder caused, when abnormal cell division results in an extra full or partial copy of chromosome 21. This extra genetic material causes the

		developmental changes and physical features of Down Syndrome'.
Dyslexia	:	Dyslexia is a common term used to describe various types of learning disabilities in reading, writing, Spelling and Math Problems.
Handicap	:	A condition resulting from, or the consequence of impairment as well as disability.
Hearing Impairment	:	HI refers to conditions in which individuals are fully or partially unable to detect or perceive at least some frequencies of sound which can typically be heard by most people.
Multiple Disabilities	:	A combination of two or more disabilities
Outreach Service	:	Offering required service in community or schools where the child with disability belongs to.
PARAKH	:	Performance Assessment, Review and Analysis of Knowledge for Holistic Development
Physical Disability	:	PD is a long-term loss or impairment of a person's physical function, resulting in a limitation of physical functioning, movements, dexterity or stamina.
Policy	:	National Education Policy or Related Policies
Project	:	Any project in service of disabilities
Rehabilitation	:	A set of measures that assist individuals who experience, or are likely to experience, disability to achieve and maintain optimal functioning in interaction with their environments"
Tadoma	:	Tadoma is a specialized communication system used for deafblind children, in which the child places the thumb on the speaker's lips and their fingers along with jawline.

*****

ABOUT THE AUTHOR
Dr. K.R. Jayachandran

Dr. K. R. Jayachandran is a Consultant Rehabilitation Practitioner, Educational Psychologist, & a Counsellor from India and a resident of Saudi Arabia since 2003. He holds Ph. D, Master's and B. Ed. Degrees, with three Diplomas from different Indian and Foreign Universities. He has specialized in 'Inclusive Education Leadership' from the University of Melbourne, Australia under the fellowship of MHRD - Govt. of India & AUSAID -Australia. He has licensed in Rehabilitation practices with Rehabilitation Council of India, New Delhi & certified in Employee Development, Assessment and Coaching from Harrison International, USA.

He had started his career as a Lecturer in Kerala in 1995, served as the Master Trainer in NCERT New Delhi under India-Australia Training and Capacity Building Program. Dr. Jay moved to Saudi Arabia as the Head of the Special Education Centre in the International Indian Public School under the Embassy of India, Riyadh. He had also served as the CBSE Counsellor for Indian Community International Schools under Indian Embassy, Saudi Arabia.

Since 2012 - 2022, Dr. Jay has been serving the Saudi Public Education Sector under Saudi Ministry of Education as the Adviser in Operation Management of various Educational programs of Tatweer Education Holding. He has also served as the Senior Consultant in Prince Sultan Center for Special Education Support Services and managed Training, Research, Inclusive Education & International Accreditation of this national center of Saudi Government. Since January 2023, he is working as the Consultant in Al-Bilad Consulting & Solutions in Riyadh, Saudi Arabia.

He has enriched the field of education as a Resource Person for SCERT Kerala, NCERT New Delhi, Universities, Colleges and different organizations in India and abroad. He has published many books, articles, research papers and presented papers in many international and national conferences in India and abroad. He is also a known speaker, Trainer & Counsellor.

Major Publications

1. *Know your Child First, Blue Rose Publishers, New Delhi*
2. *Special Education: Theories to Practice, Blue Rose Publishers, New Delhi*
3. *Moving Towards Inclusion, Prince Sultan Center for Special Education, Saudi Ministry of Education, Riyadh*
4. *Operational Manual in Special Education, Tatweer Education Holding, Saudi Ministry of Education, Riyadh*
5. *Editor, The Challenge, International Indian Public School & Special Care Center Decade Souvenir, 2005*
6. *Co-author: Essays on Women Empowerment, Editor: Dr.A. Radhakrishnan Nair, Norton Press, Chennai-Singapore.*
7. *Co-author: An insight into your Career, Editor: Kunju. C Nair, Blue Rose Publishers, New Delhi*

*****

Book available online-1
Know Your Child First

The First book of Dr. K.R. Jayachandran, 'Know Your Child First' was widely accepted by the Parents, Teachers, Social Workers, Physicians and education leaders. This book illuminates appropriate solutions for issues of children in our public education system. The topics discussed here are mainly on identifying the disorders of children, their unique educational needs, their common support services, facilities available, and various other topics related to the implementation of education and rehabilitation support services. Special Education, Inclusive Education, Counselling, Disability Rehabilitation Services, Educational & rehabilitation Management etc. are also well discussed in the book 'Know Your Child First'.

Book Review: "Know Your Child First"

"It is immensely pleasing to me that Dr. Jay has undertaken the challenging task of developing a resource book on Inclusive Education. The book 'Know Your Child First' gives an access to the writer's rich experience and expert insight into Inclusive Education. It brings together his extensive international experience as a practitioner, teacher-educator and public policy leader in various countries, providing insights and advice, which will improve the practice of those who refer to it. It will be proven to be beneficial to all the people who work in the area; from parents to professionals to administrators. I recall the special insight and empathy that he brought to his work in the years we worked together in Saudi Arabia. I am delighted to wish him every success with this extremely valuable work."

Best Regards,
Dr. Patrick John Rodgers
Senior Consultant, Education Management
New Zealand

Book available online-2
Special Education: Theories to Practice

The book **'Special Education: Theories to Practice'** is a source of guidance for quality services in special education and disability service management. The concept of Special Education, Inclusive Education, different research theories of Inclusion of Disabilities, Human Resource in disability rehabilitation, Standard of Practice in Rehabilitation, and the Process of quality services are the key areas discussed in this book. The policies, procedures, purpose, scope of services, key performance indicators (KPI), professional practice strategies, role of different professionals, responsibilities and management of support services, etc. are eloquently explained in this book.

Book Review - Special Education: Theories to Practice

"This book Special Education: Theories to Practice will be a source of guidance for quality services in disability management and special education. The rich experience attained by the author has been reflected in this book and it is crafted as one of the best books in the rehabilitation support services for the benefit of children with special needs."

I wish all the best and success for this book and author Dr. Jayachandran, and I hope it will help readers to add value in the service of children with special needs and their effective rehabilitation and education.

Best Wishes,
Dr. Shine T. J, MBBS, MD
Consultant Pediatrician, King Fahad Medical City
Ministry of Health, Riyadh, Saudi Arabia

www.ingramcontent.com/pod-product-compliance
Lightning Source LLC
LaVergne TN
LVHW061612070526
838199LV00078B/7251